The Child Within

by:

TOM HIPPS

Order this book online at www.trafford.com
or email orders@trafford.com

Most Trafford titles are also available at major online book retailers.

Printed in the United States of America.

ISBN: 978-1-4269-7193-8 (sc)
ISBN: 978-1-4269-7194-5 (e)

Trafford rev. 12/08/2011

 www.trafford.com

North America & international
toll-free: 1 888 232 4444 (USA & Canada)
phone: 250 383 6864 ♦ fax: 812 355 4082

The Child Within
ORIGINAL POEMS ABOUT POETRY

BY
TOM HIPPS

THANKS

My thanks to 8 year old Paul Nicdao, from Blackwood,
N.J., for the lettering and art work on the covers.

DEDICATION

This collection of verse about poetry, I dedicate
to all the children whose photos appear on the covers. Especially for Baul
and Joseph; for Melissa, John,
Jessica, and Julia Beth; Krissie, Brian, and Matthew; Quay,
Amanda, Rebecca, and Elizabeth; for Chris, Ryan, and
Rudolfo; for Leigh Ann and Cherilyn; for Zach and Jake;
for Nicole and Kelly; for Channon; for Juvy and
Cecelia. And for the poet who lives in each of us,
this wide eyed wonder child.

A Poem Is A Moving Thing...

DEAR READER

Poetry is a very personal thing and so much of what we get from it depends on what we bring to it, from our own life experience. Each poem may convey many meanings to different people.

Many books of poetry have been published and much has been written about the craft of writing poetry. Most writers when discussing the writing of poetry, deal with the subject almost exclusively as a technical craft, an abstract art form. This approach depersonalizes poetry and limits such work to "how to" technique. This reduces poetry to mere abstraction, just so many dead words, lines, and stanzas on so many lifeless pages.

In this collection, I attempt to explore and portray specifically some of the many facets of the individual poets' role, as well as what I view to be the purpose and thrust of poetry in general.

This work is an effort on my part to try a far different approach toward poetry; to attempt to personalize poetry by merging the craft of writing a poem, to the poem itself. Thus the techniques of writing poetry joins with the poem itself, and this merger makes them inseparable--- they become one. The poem now takes on a distinct personality all its' own. In the words of Robert Frost, it now becomes "a living thing…" When this happens, "the poem and I" may take a walk together; "the wind is a poet"; and "each face I see is a poem to me…"

Poetry may be viewed as a marriage wherein words are wedded to thoughts. Seen in this light, the poet becomes a matchmaker, his main task being to find the right word to match the right thought. The product of all his labor, the poem, is a marriage of word and thought.

Contents

THE CHILD WITHIN

THE POET WHO LIVES IN EACH OF US,
THIS WIDE EYED WONDER CHILD;
BIDS US TAME THE SAVAGE BEAST,
AND RIDE THE TEMPEST WILD.
TO GREET LIFE WITH OUTSTRETCHED ARMS,
OUR MIND, OUR HEARTS OPEN WIDE
TO ALL THINGS NEW, TO ALL THINGS YOUNG;
TO KEEP OUR DREAMS ALIVE INSIDE.
IT IS THE POET WHO LIVES IN EACH OF US,
THIS CHILD WHO LIVES WITHIN
THIS MORTAL PLACE, THIS FRAGILE HOME
OF FLESH, OF BONE, OF SKIN.
WHO SPEAKS TO US SO VERY SOFTLY,
WITH THE YOUNG INNOCENT'S VOICE:
"GO FORTH AND GREET THIS NEW BORN DAY.
REJOICE! GOOD FRIEND, REJOICE!"

MY THOUGHTS ARE LIKE A KITTEN

My thoughts are like a kitten,
they walk on padded paws;
so silently they stalk about,
first they come in, then they go out
and pause to sharpen their claws.
My thoughts are like a tiger,
locked securely in his cage;
there is so little he can see,
longing to be loose so he can run
free;
pacing, pacing in his cage,
consumed by silent rage.
My thoughts are like the piranha,
they lie lurking in the deep;
ready with their razor teeth to tear
any strange idea that wanders there;
savagely they strip it bare,
burying it in naked sleep.
My thoughts are like an eagle,
they soar to dizzy heights;
then they float on a sea of
rainbow dreams,
to sleep in their bed of feathery
schemes,
until the ending of the night.
My thoughts are like a hyena,
they just laugh at everything;
it matters little if good or bad,
if it should be funny, or very sad;
they just can't help pretending
they are always glad.

LOVELY LADY POETRY!

My very first love rejected me.
Many, many more women did the same.
But, on one truly lucky day;
I met the true love of my life.
I met someone who would one day;
become my own beloved wife.
Yes, my Lovely Lady Poetry;
she gave me lots of her time!
She taught me her rhythms;
and so much more about rhyme!
Then, Lady Poetry and I joined
our hands and our hearts.
We vowed to live together;
and to love each other;
"Until death we do part!"
Yes, Lady Poetry and I have
lived and loved in perfect harmony!
Finally; I have found my one and only
true love: the most fair;
Lovely Lady Poetry!

POETRY CHILD

Oh my poetry; you are a very precious,
precocious child!
At times, you are quite restless;
and very, very mischievous;
very often, you are temperamental and wild!
Yes; my dearly beloved child, poetry;
when I bid this old world goodbye;
I will leave no remembrance of me;
but you; my own dear child, poetry!
I will leave behind me; no progeny
for posterity!
The only portrait of me;
will be that of you; my child poetry!
Yes, I had but one child only;
and that child was you;

THE FISHERMAN POET

He carries a quality rod and reel, to reel
that Big One in; his line is strong,
as are the words of his song.
They travel far beyond the point of his pen!
His hook has a razor's sharp bite;
to penetrate; to draw blood; to excite;
to incite; and to invite.
To light the darkness; to unmask the night.
To turn blindness into deep insight.
He weighs his line with a sinker, to
plunge into the dark deep;
to awaken the naïve and innocent;
from their comfortable dream sleep!
He uses an inviting thought, as his
tasty bait; to lure the unsuspecting in,
tempting them to take a bite.
Then he reels them in from the depths of
ignorance; into the warmth of wisdom's
bright sunlight!

FISHING FOR THOUGHT

In the deep dark sea of fantasy;
in the vast ocean of thought;
the brain, an expert fisherman,
and would just love to land the Big One,
before he can get away.
To catch a fresh new thought; a real
trophy prize that has yet to be caught.
A real blue ribbon prize,
to light the fire in a hungry fisherman's
eyes!
So you bait your hook with food for thought.
And you cast your line far out;
out, out into the deep dark unknown!
Then you wait, and wait, and wait.
Waiting for a big thought fish,
to swallow your wish; hook, line, sinker.
and all. So then you can land a real prize.
You can catch a trophy thoughtfish,
to fill your empty wish dish.
This is every fisherman's; every poet's wish;
to be able to tell a true fish tale;
and to write a poetic lay.
All about the Big One, that did not
get away!

THE POET'S MANY FACES

The poet wears the face of many men;
he hides his true identity,
behind the short lines of his sharp pen.
He's a brave knight, facing a fearful
dragon, as he rides on his way.
He's a modern day David, casting his
stone, at a giant Goliath he is hoping
to slay.
Also the poet's a real Don Quixote too;
riding round jousting with alien windmills;
to fair Dulcinea, pitching his woo.
A knight; a shepherd bpy; a star-crossed
lover; are some of the many faces,
that a poet may wear.
But one thing that the poet must learn,
as he travels about anywhere;
a Goliath and a windmill are out there
waiting; just for him, they wait
somewhere!

THE POET AS JANUS

The poet, just like the god Janus,
has two faces. One face looks back on the
year just passed. So the poet tells it
just "like it was;" how it use to be.
When he takes his pen in hand, to write
his poetry.
He is a historian; referring often to
this past history!
The poet's other face, looks forward,
toward tomorrow; toward the future and
what may lay ahead.
He not only tells it like it is and
like it was; but also like it could be;
and maybe like it should be.
He's not just a fortune teller, looking
into the future; he's a sage; a seer; a
prophet; sharing his vision of how tomorrow
may be; even how it ought to be.
And the poet does all of this poetically;
through the medium that is his poetry!

A POET'S HATS

The poet may wear many hats.
He's a magician hopping about with rabbits.
He's an old hound dog, chasing black cats!
He thrusts his hand into one hat;
and abracadabra; holy moley; what is that?
With a gasp from his audience, he pulls a
kicking rabbit from his top hat!
The poet is a magician, working his magical
feats of the ledgerdemain.
In the poet's life, and in his poetry;
this magic will always remain.
The poet is an umpire.
He pulls on his hat, and dons his mask;
To call each play just the way he sees it;
this is the umpire's most important task.
He carries the rod and reel of an
expert fisherman; trying to hook the Big One,
that always gets away.
With his strong line and sharp hook,
he casts far out into the back bay!
The poet puts on his baseball hat;
then walks over to the bat rack,
to select his favorite bat.
He digs in at the plate; feet firmly planted,
he is ready for the ball.
With his smooth level swing and follow through;
he knocks it all the way over the right field wall!
To land the "Big One"; to knock the ball clear
over the wall.
This is the challenge that confronts the poet;

when the umpire makes his call;
"Play ball!"
To pull a rabbit out of a hat;
with an "abracadabra" this; and a "hocus pocus" that.
To call it just like he sees it,
on each play; on every day;
this is the role of the poet;
and the poet's poetical way!

FEEL GOOD LINES

Oh I do feel so good on this feel good day.
It would really feel good to pen a feel good lay.
Oh yes, hey man, a feel good line,
now that would really feel fine!
The grass down here is green;
the sky up there is bright blue.
Think I should try to write a feel good line,
or two! All the signs read, "yes".
All the signals say, "go!"
Down with all thoughts
that are naughts.
No is a big N-O!
On this feel good day, I would feel more fine;
if I could compose a good feel good line.
A good poetic line to match my feel fine day.
The sun up there in his heaven, is in
his sunny mood.
The bees buzzing through the trees,
have a fuzzy, buzzy bee attitude!
For this once in a lifetime scene,
do you know what I mean?
I have so much feel fine, feel good gratitude!
The birds are on a lark!
The flowers in the park are dancing.
To the wind's amorous romancing!

KEEP ON SINGING

Keep on singing, she told me, as she
hurried on her way. And being like a bird
with a clipped wing;
since I can't fly; I can only sing!
Oh to be a bird; not only could I be
singing; whenever I felt the urge to fly,
I would be off and winging!
Not being a bird, I have no wing.
So all that I can do is sing.
Sing with my tongue and with my pen.
This gives me a voice; to celebrate life;
to rejoice. To invite my fellowmen to
come on along; and join me in my song!
My tongue is my voice; my pen is my wing.
With my tongue and my pen, I can fly,
and I can sing. For with his tongue and
with his pen; the poet gives voice
to his fellow men!

DEEP DRINKER

The poet, being a deep drinker, he drinks
in beauty night and day.
Such intoxicating draughts of beauty,
inspiring many a poet's lyrical lay.
Much drinking, the thought is, leads to
deep thinking.
Such deep drinking and deep thinking,
these are identical twins.
When these twins collaborate,
beauty always wins.
The poet drinks deeply, from love's
overflowing stream.
From these depths of love, the poet fishes
to catch an elusive dream.
The poet's wish: a rare dream fish,
to fill his empty dream dish!

NAKED POET

The poet stands before you in the raw;
stark naked and stripped bare.
He stands there for all prying eyes to see.
For any and every interested party.
To theorize. To dissect and to analyze,
his poetry. Just how can this be?
The poet lays out his brain;
inviting the reader, "Come pick it clean."
The reader asks the poet,
"What is on your mind? What do you know?
What is it you mean?"
The poet lays his heart out on the table.
Here is what I feel in my heart.
You are very welcome to cut it up;
to tear it apart.
From my heart you will learn the real;
the true me.
You will learn what I care most about.
What means the very most to me.
What I strongly feel. What to me is real.
Here I stand before you; stark naked
and stripped bare.
I only ask, with my mind and with my heart,
oh please do take good care!
For this is the only brain and heart I have.
So to me, it is priceless; and a thing
most rare!

I AM A POET

I am a poet and I write the poems
that people read.
My poetry serves their deepest need.
I plant in their heads,
thought's fragile seed.
Their thirst I quench.
Their hunger I feed.
I am a poet and I write,
the poems that many people recite.
My verses stir; uplift; and excite!
I light a raging fire at mid-day.
I plant a dewy dream at midnight!
I am a poet and I write the poetry
that people remember.
My verse awakens yesterday's cold ember.
It bring a fresh bouquet from May;
to their cold December!
I am a poet. I write the poetry
that unlocks a closed mind;
that sets the caged spirit free!
Free to be reborn; to live; to love;
to enjoy the liberty to be!

PO EM*

Poem,
She sat by her window, and waited for him.
Her own dear sweet Prince Charming.
Her very own knight in shining armor.
To come riding her way,
Her own pet dragons to slay!
To charm her and disarm her.
To sweep her far away.
To a land where life is pure poetry.
And each day, a lyrical romantic lay!
*In memory of Emily Dickinson…

MY NAME IS POETRY

On the fleet wings of song,
straight to you I fly.
I soar to the top of the highest hills;
I climb the mountains of the sky!
Over lush meadows; down valleys green;
I serenade the earth; with my
rhythmic lullaby.
I an your very own nightingale;
come to set your caged heart free.
My name is poetry!
On the printed page,
that is my stage;
watch me jump see me leap and plea.
As I perform for you; as I dance you you;
my own poetical ballet!
On the slow feet of a turtle,
I crawl along my way.
On the paws of a kitten or a puppy;
I love to frolic in play!
On the fleet feet of the cheetah;
I chase down my prey!
On the swift hooves of the stallion;
I race the wind both night and day!
I am poetry. Please come with me now.
We will sing; and dance; and play!

I AM POETRY

I am poetry. Hear my heart beat,
to the rhythmic symmetry of my feet.
This poetical, musical symphony;
I carry on my feet of poetry!
I am poetry, and my romantic sigh;
is the softest kiss of a lullaby;
the laugh of a happy child at play;
the tender touch of a lyrical lay!
I am poetry; open; high spirited
and free!
I breathe the fresh air of liberty!
I am poetry, and my beat;
is the pounding rhythm of the street;
the sound of the souls of a million feet!
I am poetry. Can you see me?
Do you hear me?

You shall above all things be glad
and young. For if you're young,
whatever life you wear it will be-
come you; and if you are glad what-
ever's living will yourself become.."
--- e.e. cummings

MY HEART'S YOUNG ROAD

My heart's young road reaches out for
the sunshine, its' thirsty tongue
lapping up the miles;
My heart's new day stretches up for
the sunlight, its' hungry mouth
devouring the smiles.
My heart's fresh song climbs for the
treetops, its' childlike melody just
learning to fly;
My heart's first love ascends the
mountain, its' childish trust
embracing the sky.
My heart's youthful dream plants
tender tomorrows, explores virgin lands
beyond restless seas;
My hearts eager hope plants welcome-
ing rainbows, on happy horizons
framing bright memories.

WORD BIRD

Words are to thoughts
what wings are to birds;
if you would climb to a
mountain top,
just give a thought a word.
Thoughts are to a word
what birds are to a wing;
if you would soar above the
clouds, just teach a word
to sing.
Wed a single word to a
single thought,
and you exceed the power of
a king.

y poets are the ones who speak
to me with clarity and innocence,
and beauty…"
--- Helen Hayes

THE WIND IS A POET

The wind is a poet in his own
right;
waving at nodding branches,
laughing at a dancing kite;
whispering to lurking shadows,
skipping to childrens' play;
anxious for the happy sunrise,
eager to start the day.
The wind is a poet in his own
time;
copying from a songbird a good
beginning line;
borrowing from the ocean a
mariner's nautical rhyme;
some rhythm from a dancer's feet,
some volume from a waterfall;
the melody of a child's laughter,
a poetic gift for all.

THE BUTTERFLY POET

On lyric wings the butterfly
serenades the day,
and tells the secrets of the
night, in her own windswept
way.
She writes her verse upon
the sky,
as she lingers on a breeze;
then with a flourish she
signs her name,
and reads it to the trees.

A RIDDLE IN RHYME

I have feet but I cannot walk.
You cannot hear me, but I can talk.
I can lay and yet I never sleep.
Sometimes I laugh and then again I weep.
I can sing but I have no voice.
Still my songs make many sad hearts rejoice.
I have thoughts but I cannot think.
I may grow yet I seldom do shrink.
An artist, I neither point nor draw.
And yet my pictures quite often inspire
much awe.
I have a beginning, but where I end
is something on which you cannot depend.
I can swing, leap, dance, and play.
Even on a very cold or a very hot day.
When I am most wise, I may be very glad.
Often when I am happy, I am the most sad.
I am at home almost anywhere.
In joy and happiness, or in deep despair.
If I am angry, it means I do care.
The one thing I like to do most is to share.
Just who I am may be a dark mystery?
And yet it is just as simple as A, B, C.
So my good friend, let me introduce you to me.
My name, my friend, is poetry.
"Poets are mad," someone once said.
I am not quite sure of just what this person

POETS ARE MAD

"Poets are mad," someone once said.
I am not quite sure of just what this person
meant nor of his or her intent? Still, I
think this statement quite true;
oh yes, I really do. I do
like the idea that poets are mad. In these mad
days, anyone worth being called a poet should
very well be mad. When it's open season on reason,
not to be mad at the way things are,
would at best be most bizarre,
not to mention poetic treason.
Only a fool; a masochist; a glutton would be
content with our present state;
could be resigned to our current fate.
This would be the ultimate crime,
with no reason and no rhyme.
In this mad season we need someone mad to
lead the way.
We madly need a mad poet for this mad day.

"A poet is somebody who feels…
Poetry is feeling--- not knowing or
believing or thinking. The moment you
feel, you're nobody-but-yourself…"
--- e.e. cummings

SOMEBODY WHO FEELS

A poet is somebody who feels and who
expresses his feelings poetically.
If you would be real and have your
poetry be real, know what you feel,
and say what you feel; not what
someone else may know or say or feel.
Your feeling is you; it belongs only
to you.
Know your feelings and know yourself;
to yourself and your feelings you will
be true.
Poetry is not in knowing or in wanting
to or getting to know.
It is not in what you think you know
or what you know you do know--- oh no.
You can be taught to know, you know?
Nor is poetry in what you may think,
or in what you think you think.
You can be taught what to think and
even how to think, you see.
Just to think is not poetry.
Poetry is not in learning or writing;
nor in the mind or the brain, that's so.
You can be taught what to learn, how to
learn; what to write and how to write;
how to speak and what to say, oh yes,
it is so. But, you cannot be taught
what to feel and how to feel; that's
the one part of yourself that is your-
self and true and real--- what you feel.

But, the world would have you be un-
real; unlike yourself; it would have
you think and learn and know and
write and feel; just like it thinks
and learns and knows and writes and
feels. If you would be a poet, and
somebody new; somebody real; someone
true--- be something fresh and alive,
only you. To be flesh and blood liv-
ing poetry; be free to be free and
real--- then feel, only feel.

"Poetry is an angler. It hooks
you in a second. It reels you in
like a fish. Poetry is a very
lively thing…"
--- Myron Klutts (Grade 8)

A CHAMPION ANGLER

The poet is a real live Jonah,
gone fishing for a whale;
trying to catch the big one who
always get away;
now wouldn't that be some
fisherman's tale?
The poet is a fanatic fisherman,
armed with bait and his trusty
fishing pole;
he's always on a sharp lookout,
before he casts his hook out,
for the very best fishing hole.
The poet is a champion angler,
casting off into the deep;
hoping to land the slippery
wishfish, where all the big
fish sleep.
The poet has gone fishing,
to hook the big one who got away;
his sharp hook baited with a
tempting word to land a slippery
thought with his poetic word play.
He could hook himself a trout,
and you just never do know,
reel in a pot of gold with his
own rainbow.
And the poet is always angling
for an angel fish;
now that would really cook up
some heavenly dish.
What more could a poet wish?

POETRY IS BLUE

Poetry is the blue of blue skies,
a blue fire dancing in blue eyes;
bluebirds nesting in green trees,
bluefish swimming in blue seas.
Poetry is the blue of bluedays,
blue flowers blooming in green Mays;
blue poets singing to bluemoons,
bluesongs springing in green Junes.
Poetry is the blue of blue wings,
blue buds swinging in green springs;
blue Jacks playing with blue Jills,
blue Jills tumbling down green hills.
Poetry is the blue of March wind,
and April rain;
bluegrass waving on a green plain;
Blue dreams waking to bluedawns,
bluebells blueming on green lawns.
Poetry is the blue of true,
as in true friend,
true love, true blue.
Poetry is the blue of free,
flying in blue sky,
swimming in blue sea;
free is for you as free is for me,
the blue of poetry.

"POETRY? YUCKY!"

To freckle faced Chucky,
poetry is, "Yucky!'
To bombastic Billy,
it is just plain silly.
To pig-tailed Crissy,
it is only for a sissy.
To willy nilly Millie,
it is too darn frilly.
To sweetreat Pete,
poetry is simply too sweet.
To harum scarum Harry,
it is something for a fairy.
To looney tooney Larry,
it's wild and hairy--- scarey!
To chic fancy Nancy,
it is only for a pansie.
To Sonny the Streak,
it's a real freak-
out scene;
d'ya dig what I mean?

"My breath--- this is what I call
this song, for it is just as
necessary for me to sing it as it
is to breathe. I will sing this
song, a song that is strong..."
--- Orpingalik (Eskimo)

DON QUIXOTE, POET

Give a poet a pen and quicker than you can
say, "Dulcinea", he climbs upon his high
horse and rides off into the sunrise,
looking for windmills to fight.
Give a poet a pad and faster than you can
say, "Sancho Panza", he hops on his hobby
horse and gallops off into the sunset,
out of sight.
The poet, a would be Don Quixote, strides
out into the world brandishing his sharp pen;
he jests and he parries with his fellowmen.
This mere flesh and blood mortal, he;
daily jousts with deity.
And grappling with the gods,
he tries his very best to even out the odds;
or at the very least reach up and pull down
a small piece of heaven for man,
the poor lost beast!
Poets imagine they are a real life Don
Quixote, jousting with alien windmills,
wrestling with adversity; in reality they are
the windmills, turning to every gust of wind,
standing mute before each Quixotic thrust.
A pathetic poetic paean to dust!

CAT AND MOUSE

In poetry, the poet is a cat stalking a timid
mouse;
he plays his poetic game of hide and seek
all about the house.
From the bedroom, to the bathroom;
from the bathroom to the kitchen,
he hunts his wary prey.
And then he traps it in the kitchen.
Oops! There's one that got away.
Sometimes in the world of poetry,
even a mouse will have his way.
And the cat is left to wait and hunt
another day.

SEARCHING FOR WINDMILLS

While out searching for windmills
one day,
a real life Don Quixote came
riding my way.
I told him I needed a windmill
to fight,
that I wanted to battle the wrong,
to defend what was right.
Then he bade me mount his trusty
steed,
and the two of us rode off at
quixotic speed.
We rode and we rode until my
bottom was sore,
and we stopped quite abruptly
right at my own front door.
And to my astonishment,
to my very great surprise,
there stood a giant windmill,
right before my very eyes.
Then out of the farthest corner
of my nearest eye,
a fire breathing dragon
I spotted nearby.
Both a windmill and a dragon,
why no poet could ask for more.
So, I armed myself
with my sharpest pen,
and then marched off to war.

THUS SAITH THE GREAT POET

In the writing of poetry
there is no end;
and too much poetry is tiresome
to the hand that wields the pen.
Amen!
"There's nothing worse
than a domesticated poet..."
--- Stanley Kunitz

HEAR ME KNOCKING?

Hear me knocking at your heart,
my friend?
I am but a poor poet
seeking sanctuary for a time;
may I please come in
and share with you
my rhyme?
Hear me pounding on your head,
good friend?
I am but a poor poem
seeking refuge for awhile;
may I please come in
and share with you a smile?
Feel me scratching on your ear,
dear friend?
I am but a poor singer
singing my song;
trying hard to get under
your skin;
may I please come in?
It could very well be
that my poetic lay,
will brighten your way,
will make your day?
There is just one hitch,
friend:
you have got to let me
come in.
"So for poetry, the concern is
not to arrive at a definition
and close the book, but to
arrive at an experience…"
--- John Ciardi

"I have been one acquainted with
the night…"
--- Robert Frost

YOU POETS

You poets,
left to say the final amen
upon my cold stone,
over my still bone;
take time to pen:
With my verse,
I strove to remove just one
minute of curse,
from this accursed race of
men.
With each painful pen stroke
I sought to lift life's
heavy yoke,
for only one hour.
I tried to stay for but one
small minute,
the mighty fist of power.
With each lyrical lay,
I would halt for one day
the sure march of time;
to lift one small sin
from my fellowmen;
to forgive them just one
crime.
With my poetry,
I hoped to draw from the cup
of misery,
one bitter tear;
to soothe one broken heart,
to remove one weighty fear.

With each poem, I would
relieve some of life's sharp
pain, from those so sorely
grieved.
And if I did give one lost
soul, one reason to live,
perhaps this poet will not
have lived, nor have died in
vain

"Come let us roam the night to-
gether singing…"
--- Langston Hughes

𝒦.𝒪. 𝒦𝒥𝒩𝒢

The poet's words:
sharp sledgehammer punches
well aimed to deflate overblown
windbags,
well planted to chop overgrown
egos down to mere mortal size.
Like Joe Louis in his prime
they keep on coming at you,
bringing their bad news:
this just might be your time,
brother, sister;
Mrs., mister?
They're coming, coming;
always coming,
looking for an opening;
for just the right moment
to play truth and consequences,
in poetical sequences.
Stalking, sparring;
jabbing, jarring,
they trap you in a corner
with a crisp 1,2,3 combo;
then they set you up for a
say-goodnight-now blow.
With a solid uppercut
flush on the chin,
they score a clean kayo.
The poet is one mean mother
of a muse,
who doesn't aim to amuse;

does not intend to confuse
the issue---
he does not want to kiss you.
Simply stated it all boils
down to:
you stand up tall and proud;
you speak up clear and loud
until you've had your say,
in your own unique way.

"As soon as a poet affiliates
himself with power, he dooms
himself…"
--- Stanley Kunitz

LET ME HUNGER

Let me hunger!
Let me thirst!
May I never know the feeling of
content.
May I be intent
on never being satisfied.
Let me always feel that want
inside,
that will not, that cannot be
denied!
I hunger! I thirst!
I have not yet died!
A poet well fed,
is a poet securely dead;
a glutton who lives only to eat,
who grovels at the powerful's feet;
a mad dog who only wants to gnaw
his bone,
when there is far better meat to
feed on.
A poet well fed,
of necessity makes his bed
with the sweet scented whores of
success; with the well groomed
pimps of excess.
While the well fed go a whoring,
let me instead go warring!
A poet well fed,
is a coddled pet so easily led

on the leash of power;
the well groomed, well dressed,
well trained, polished man-of-the-
hour.
Such a poet, so well fed,
so very easily trained and led,
is oh so very, very comfortably
dead!

"Do not go gentle into that dark
night… Rage, rage, against
the dying of the light…"
---Dylan Thomas

I RAGE

I rage! I rage!
Against the ruthless tyranny
of a blank page,
I rage!
I rage! I rage!
Against the witless agony
of a blind mind,
each all-of-one-kind,
I rage!
I rage! I rage!
Against the crazed babble
of a foolish pen;
the worthless rabble,
this race called men.
I rage, and rage, and
I rage again!
I rage! I rage!
Against the unyielding word,
the unbending line;
against the heave yoke
of Old Father Time,
I rage! I rage!

THE UMPIRE POET

Give me a poet for an umpire every
time;
he calls it just like he sees it
right on down the line.
Fair or foul, foul or fair,
to him it's all the same;
he calls it like it is,
every single game.
He does not care what team is
at bat;
he's oblivious to the crowd's
wild roar;
it matters not the inning of the
game--- he never takes note of
the score.

DOODLEBUG POET

Doodlebug, doodlebug rolling along,
doodlebug, doodlebug sing me your song.
I'm just a lowly doodlebug rolling along,
just a simple doodlebug singing my song.
I sit on a pile of it rolling a ball of it,
just a lowly doodlebug rolling along,
nothing but a doodlebug singing my song.
Doodlebug, doodlebug why do you roll?
When you are knee deep in it,
and you're up to your eyeballs in it;
you've got a big bellyful of it,
oh just why do you roll?
"Yes, I'm just a little doodlebug a
rolling along,
a simple doodlebug singing my song.
If you're over your head in it,
and you can't stand the smell of it,
let alone the taste of it;
yet you're stuck in the midst of it,
what else is there to do with it
but roll, roll, roll?"
Doodlebug, doodlebug have you no goal?
Is that all you can do with it
just roll, roll, roll?
"I'm just a lowly doodlebug rolling along,
nothing but a doodlebug singing my song.
Since I don't like the smell of it,
can't even stand the taste of it;
I've got a big bellyful of it,
and there's too much to pack away of it;
there is nothing else to do with it
just roll, roll, roll."

Doodlebug, doodlebug rolling along,
doodlebug, doodlebug keep singing
your song:
"I'm just a lowly doodlebug rolling along,
just a little doodlebug singing my song.
As long as I sing my song of it,
then the taste of it, the smell of it,
will not be too strong for me to get along;
and this simple little doodlebug can
keep right on rolling along."

"A thing of beauty is a joy
forever…"
--- John Keats

BEAUTY

Beauty is the poet's mistress.
From his cradle to his grave,
the poet serves his mistress
beauty,
as her devoted obedient slave.
He offers her his homage and
tribute;
composing for her his lyrical
lays.
The poet immortalizes his mistress
beauty,
with his poetical paeans of ador-
ing praise.
Beauty is the poet's true love,
and to beauty,
the poet is always forever true.
She is his lover,
and his own very best friend;
he gives his life to her,
right up to the end;
the poet keeps his vow:
"yes I will!
Yes I do!'

A POET I THINK*

Who will pick up the pieces of our
shattered world? A poet I think.
Who will pick up the splinters of
our broken lives? a poet I think.
Who will make us whole for he can
see things whole? A poet I think
may fill this role.
Who has the gift of joy?
Who speaks with clarity and vision;
with innocence and beauty?
A poet I think.
Who can give to man something worth
imitating, an ideal to strive for?
A poet I think.

       * For Helen Hayes ...

"The man bent over his guitar,
a shearsman of sorts… They said,
"you have a blue guitar, you do not
play things as they are." The man
replied, "Things as they are are
changed upon the blue guitar…"
--- Wallace Stevens

ON THE DEATH OF A POET*

There is much more sadness in the
death of a poet, than there is
in the fall of a king;
it's much easier to fill an empty
throne, than to find some voice
to sing.
All you need is to polish a dusty
crown then fit it to some empty
head;
but how do you replace a silent
voice, for with the poet,
the pen is dead.
And yet, throughout the ages, the
poet's banner flies high;
while the king's trumpets lie silent,
and his name's but a whispered sigh.
The poet, his sword drawn and ready,
marches on through the pages of rhyme;
while the mighty kings of history,
lay dead in their cold tomb of time.
For whenever a poem is read,
and someone heeds its' call,
a David marches forth to do battle,
and a Goliath waits to fall.
For the pen of the poet is sharper

that the mighty sword of time;
and his rapier thrusts pierce the
centuries, with each poetic rhyme!
*For "Sonny Boy Wlls, known to some
as Allie Egan Walls, Jr., and to others
as "The Poet" --- in Savannah, Georgia…

"I'd rather learn from one bird
how to sing than teach ten
thousand stars how not to dance..
--- e.e. cummings

THE PUGILIST POET

Poetry!
It really hits you man,
right here in the gut;
like a Muhammed Ali quick
one-two combo flush on the chin
it knocks you right out!
And poetry is in!
Poetry!
Do you dig?
It really comes on big.
With a jab in the face,
like Joe Louis punch;
it takes you out for lunch.
Poetry's a real Joe Palooka;
with a bazooka blow,
that scores a clean kayo.

THE GRAMMARIAN POET

As grammarian:
the poet is not disturbed
by the undotted "i"
nor the uncrossed "t";
Quixotic, he wars against
the "in" of inevitability.

THE PEN POET

As a pen:
the poet pricks
comfortable behinds;
he prods sleepy minds.
"Wake up!"
He punctures inflated rears:
"Bottoms up!

"A poem is a mirror walking down a
strange street…
--- Lawrence Ferlinghetti

TOMORROW POETS

Today belongs to the lovers,
for all lovers today is their
song.
For them there are no tomorrows,
all is right and nothing is wrong.
Let them love while love is in
season,
while their hearts and their love
is still young.
There will be time left for reason,
but today their song must be sung.
Today their dreams must be planted,
their tomorrows, today they must sow.
Today love is planting her garden,
that only tomorrow will grow.
Tomorrow belongs to the poets,
let them sing of tomorrow today.
Let them tell us of worlds that
lie waiting,
when our world has faded away.
Let them build a dream that will
guide us,
through lands we now do not know.
Let them plant a hope to sustain us,
whenever and wherever we go.
Let them sing us a song
well remember,
as our memory slips slowly away.
May it cheer the long night before us,
as we live our tomorrow,
today.

A POEM'S A LEMON LOLLIPOP

A poem is a lemon lollipop you have to
lick for awhile,
if you would taste the sweetness of
the sun's friendly smile.
A poem's a licorice gumdrop,
let it sleep beneath your tongue;
if you would taste the melody
of a night that is still young.

"Every time a poem is written,
it is written not by cunning,
but by belief…"
--- Robert Frost

MOD POETRY

In modern poetry (so called),
to be vague is in vogue;
to insist on, to persist in
having no title, is your entitle;
(sounds much more mischievous,
if you make it devious).
In today's poesy (so called),
to be slick is the trick,
(you need a gimmick, quick);
keep a card up your sleeve,
(do you believe that,
a rabbit in your hat?).
The mystical rites of ledgerde-
main must always maintain,
(omit the word "maintain",
insert instead remain).
In modern musery (so called),
longevity has preference over
brevity;
the idea to go onandonandonandon,
out with a sigh here,
there emit a groan;
(cancel out "groan" and substitute moan).
In now poetry (so called),
the really "in style is free
style, no-style.
Now today mod poets insist that
rhyming is simple simon;
why it's even a capital crime
to ever commit a rhyme;
not to rhyme;

not to rhyme is chic,
to rhyme is not macho,
(would you please pass the nacho);
it's so weak,
(like kissing your cousin on the
cheek).
"The sound is gold in the ore…"
--- Robert Frost

MOD POETRY (Contd.)

As any fool knows,
poetry is only prose,
dressed up in its' Sunday-go-to-
meeting-clothes;
and prose is pure poetry,
to the mod poet wannabe.
These mod poets, so in, so now;
so hip, so with it, so cool;
to hear them tell it, they don't
dig jive; hey man, they're real
bad, dad! They're nobody's fool.
In contemporary poetry,
(so called),
just go hog wild,
sweet honey child;
just do your own thing,
swing it and wing it;
(in contemporary lingo),
just let it all go,
like so:
go
tfel
go
right
fo

p
u
go
d

o

w

n

r o

a go u

...d n

It (poetry) is a very living thing.
It is as life itself..."
--- Robert Frost

A POEM IS A MOVING THING

A poem is a moving thing:
a leaping,
swaying,
skipping thing;
a poem is a swinging thing,
a prancing,
dancing,
playing thing;
a poem is a springing thing,
a winging,
singing,
song with wings.
A poem is a touching thing:
a feeling,
clasping,
clinging thing;
a poem is a grasping thing,
a clutching,
holding,
keeping thing;
a poem's an emerging thing,
a wind penned,
sunscript,
mist kissed thing.
A poem is a welcome thing:
a trusting,
hoping,
open thing;
a poem is a laughing thing,
a smiling,
warming,
happy thing;

a poem is a sunrise thing,
a sunsculpt,
dewdrop,
fledgling thing;
a poem is a sunset thing,
a moonstruck,
starburst,
dream time thing.
A poem is an awakening.
A poem is a growing thing:
a sowing,
sprouting,
pruning thing;
a poem is a budding thing,
a blooming,
ripening,
bearing thing.
A poem is a becoming thing,
a seeking,
probing,
finding thing;
a poem is a giving thing,
a working,
reaping,
enduring thing.
A poem is a living thing:
a blood born,
brain bought
heart hewn thing;
a poem is a loving thing,
a daring,
caring,
sharing thing.
A poem is a harvesting…

THE POET, A DON QUIXOTE

The poet, a real flesh and blood Don Quixote,
marches boldly into the fray.
He has Goliath; Godzilla; a dragon; and a
windmill waiting. To the poet, there is
always a monster to slay.
Like Dirty Harry, the poet is just waiting,
for any beast to "make his day!"
The poet hungers to feast, on the beast, you
could say. This is the poet's poetic purpose.
This is the poet's poetical way.
The poet is always very well prepared;
well armed with his sharp trusty pen:
To wrestle with the demons of man's nature;
to spar with his fellow men.
With his faithful pen, and a piece of paper;
the poet is ever ready to cut a caper.
The poet is also a magician, a
sorcerer of sound; stirring up his
bewitching brew of sorcerers' stew.
He seasons quite liberally with meta-
phor and simile, in concocting his
magical recipe. Then he adds a little
reason to his rhyme and the result may
very well be a potent poetic potion.
But the poet is much more than chef,
matchmaker and sorcerer. In his writ-
ing and his daily life, he must act
out the role of gladiator, a modern
David battling the Goliaths that con-
front him; like Jacob, he wrestles
with angels; as a Daniel he has to
fight fierce lions in their own den.
A present day Noah, he is forced to
desert the safety of his ark and

venture out on treacherous seas; on a
perilous journey that invites daily
conflict, that provokes constant
challenge. This travel on "the road
not taken", in the words of Frost,
"makes all the difference." Cast
in this role, the poet at his best
is the classic Quixotic figure, a
knight jousting with the alien wind-
mills that block his path at every
turn.

Helen Hayes in her book, <u>A Gift
Of Joy</u>, says "only he(the poet) can
grasp the splinters and make a new
wholeness that does not yet exist. Who
will pick up the pieces of our dam-
aged world? A poet I think…" This
is really the role of the poet: to
grasp the splinters and pick up the
pieces. From these splinters of mean-
ing, these pieces of experience, these
fragments of life--- the poet tries to
construct a wholeness that will give
some sense of purpose to life; and
hopefully, scatter a little beauty
along the way.

--- Tom Hipps

"The hours rise up putting off stars
and it is dawn
into the street of the sky light walks
scattering poems…
--- e.e. cummings

THE CHILD WITHIN

THE POET WHO LIVES IN EACH OF US,
THIS WIDE EYED WONDER CHILD;
BIDS US TAME THE SAVAGE BEAST,
AND RIDE THE TEMPEST WILD.
TO GREET LIFE WITH OUTSTRETCHED ARMS,
OUR MIND, OUR HEARTS OPEN WIDE
TO ALL THINGS NEW, TO ALL THINGS YOUNG;
TO KEEP OUR DREAMS ALIVE INSIDE.
IT IS THE POET WHO LIVES IN EACH OF US,
THIS CHILD WHO LIVES WITHIN
THIS MORTAL PLACE, THIS FRAGILE HOME
OF FLESH, OF BONE, OF SKIN.
WHO SPEAKS TO US SO VERY SOFTLY,
WITH THE YOUNG INNOCENT'S VOICE:
"GO FORTH AND GREET THIS NEW BORN DAY.
REJOICE! GOOD FRIEND, REJOICE!"

POEMS ARE PLAYFUL CHILDREN

Poems are playful children
who like to play hide and seek:
"Ready or not, here I come.
No fair now to take a peek."
Poems like to play tag,
challenging, "Catch me, if you
can--- I'm it."
And around and around the
mulberry bush,
the weasel gives the monkey
a fit.
A poem is a playful child
who just loves to dance and
sing;
it drops the handkerchief in
the fall,
and hopskotches in the spring!

TO THE POET

To the poet:
that still small voice
who is always near;
who speaks to each of us
in a voice loud and clear;
if we will only listen,
if we still can hear.
To all of my closest friends,
and to my own family;
to all of these, to all of you,
who mean so much to me:
To: Linda, Evelyn, Luzviminda,
and Tammy; for Dick and Stan;
Ed and Sid; Ralph and Dwight;
for Terri and Mary; and for my
sister, Mary Lou.
For the poet who lives in all of you,
the poet I love in you.

A POETS' LULLABY

My heart has a thousand songs to sing
to the moon,
to the stars,
to the sky.
And I have a thousand gifts to bring:
no gold or silver
from the treasure of kings,
but a poets' lullaby.

POETRYS' PAGES

Each face I see
is a poem to me.
Each time penned line
a story in rhyme.
A saga of the ages
for poetrys' epic pages.
"In poems, our earth's wonders
are windowed through words... A
good poem must haunt the heart..."
--- Peter Kelso (Age 11)

A POETS' CREED

Into the wind I stride,
with a will that wont be denied,
I straddle the tempest and ride.
Into the suns' hot eye,
a moth to the flame I fly,
trembling I reach for the sky.
Into the darkness of night,
seeking one glimmer of light,
blindly I grope for insight.
Into the tempest I go,
tossed by the storms to and fro,
forward with lifes' ebb and flow.

AS POET

As poet:
it isn't the isn't
that disturbs me the most;
it is the sacred is
we wine, we dine,
we host, we toast.
As poet:
it isn't the will not
that most distresses me;
it is the holy will,
we serve as Deity.

THE POET MUST

The poet must
cut across the grain of life
with a sharp knife.
The poet must
prune the dead branches
that the tree may grow high;
climbing the sky
until it makes friends
of sun and bird,
and lends a wing
to some fledgling word.

y poets have the gift of joy,
they are the ones who can see things whole,
who can sense and comprehend the vast scheme
that has been designed for us…"
--- Helen Hayes

ON THE HOUSE

Flesh of my flesh I give to you,
such a gift as this mortal is
heir to:
the poets' lot,
a paupers' plot;
hard muscle of mind,
lean tendon of thought
to fleshen bare bone;
strong sinew of soul
to feed on.
Blood of my blood I offer you,
this hemlock cup
a poet must sup;
dregs of dust
in this vessel of rust;
a sorcerers' brew,
this pot-luck stew.
Grapes of hope hang heavy
on the vine,
drowning despair in the
spirit lifting wine.
Sweat of my sweat,
bread of my brow;
bone of my bone
I break with you now.

THE POET QUIXOTIC

In these dark ages of the despotic,
in a world grown so chaotic,
you may dispense with the exotic,
send me a poet Quixotic.
In this savage time when tyranny
is the rule,
when freedom is the tyrants'
bloody tool,
send me just one Quixotic fool.

"The most exciting movement in nature is
not progress, advance, but expansion and
contraction, the opening and shutting
of the eye, the hand, the heart, the
mind…"
--- Robert Frost

OPEN DOOR

Open your door wide,
invite the storm inside.
Learn something of heaven's
intent;
feel the unbridled fury of
firmament!
Bid the darkness come in;
let curious fingers explore
timid skin.
Feel the stirrings of a
universe within!
Open your door wide,
welcome the stranger outside.
Know something of earth's
mortality,
feel the unharnessed anger of
deity!
Throw open your arms to
your plight;
cling to the last faint flicker
of light.
You lovers. You poets---
embrace the night!

BLOODWINE

Pour a glass of warm bloodwine,
come join me in a rare vintage line;
shall we sit down with the gods to dine?
As we break this loaf of fresh heartbread,
and feed upon what some poet has said;
let us savor such food of the gods
that we have read.
Come you thirsty! You hungry come!
We resurrect the dead!

THESE ARE THE RHYMES

These are the rhymes
that pry
into men's souls,
that spy
on men's souls,
that sigh
for men's souls.
Hopefully these rhymes
never try men's souls,
never lie to men's souls.
These are the rhymes
that ask why
of men's souls,
that ply
men's souls,
that vie
for men's souls.
Although these rhymes
may cry for men's souls;
hopefully these rhymes
will live and die in men's souls.

THE REBEL POET

This poet is proud to be a revel.
I revel in rebelry.
I rebel with revelry.
Hell yes! I'm a hellion,
for rebellion.
This rebel poet's rebel yell:
I rebel! I rebel! I rebel!

EACH DAY

Each day my eyes grow blind,
each day the more I see;
each day I am bound,
each day I am set free.
Each day I am born and die,
each day I die and live;
each day in death we have life,
each day in life we give,
Each day I look at life,
each day death looks at me;
each day I lift my pen,
each day is poetry.

"The height of all poetic thinking,
that attempt to say matter in terms
of spirit, and spirit in terms of
matter..."
--- Robert Frost

WELCOME

Welcome into my dreams;
oh wont you please just step
inside?
For you, the door is open wide.
Here the skies are always blue,
and there's a rainbow just for you;
life is always what it seems,
in my dreams.
Welcome into my heart;
wont you please step right in-
side?
For you, the door is open wide.
Together we will share mirth and
song,
chase the weary blues along;
a fresh new day is eager to start,
in my heart.
Welcome into my poem;
Oh wont you please come on inside?
For you, the door is open wide.
We will share some lyrical lay,
just to pass the time of day;
life is one paean to poesy,
in my poetry.
Welcome into my life;
for you, the door is open wide.
Please do come in!
Just step inside.....

DOWN HERE

Down here in this desert,
where we mortal poets are stewing;
I cannot help but wonder what
the gods on Olympus are brewing?
Down here in this jungle,
where we poets are living and dying;
I wonder just what is in the pan,
the immortals up there are frying?

MARRIAGE

A thought goes courting an
interesting word;
romancing an attractive adjective,
pursuing a lonely noun,
a bashful verb.
And who knows, maybe eventually,
they will enter into blissful
matrimony?
Now mind you, only the right word
will ever do;
one that will be faithful,
devoted, and true;
long after they have promised:
"Yes, I will!
Yes, I do!
A word starts wooing an
unwed thought;
propositioning a preposition,
catching a subject and being caught;
teasing a conjunction,
flirting with a cute phrase,
teaching a lesson and being taught.
What a joy! Such a thrill!
When the word asks:
"Will you marry me?"
And the thought answers:
"Yes, I will!"

POETPOURRI

Shake some simile in your pot;
stir, stir, stir a lot.
Now add some meaty metaphor;
simmer, simmer, simmer more.
Next, just a taste of rhyme
to season;
and you add a little touch of
reason.
You have cooked up a gourmet
recipe,
a tasty dish of poetpourri.

"A poet must be an adversary spirit
in the modern world…"
--- Stanley Kunitz

THE POET'S HAND

The poets' hand with rapier pen,
jests and jousts with his fellowmen.
With many a quick thrust,
and clever feint,
he fences with them
both sinner and saint.
With his poetical parry and
his playful pun,
he prods and he jokes
just having his fun.
With his poison pen and
deadly tome,
he pierces thin skin,
cutting straight to the bone.
With his sharp wily wit,
scoring a direct hit,
he drives his point straight home.

ON GUARD

On guard:
keep your lance poised and steady;
keep your saddle girth fastened
real tight;
keep your hand on your sword
and ever ready,
in midday and even at midnight.
There's a windmill waiting for you;
just for you it waits,
brave knight.
On guard:
keep your slingshot always with you,
stone in hand, and ready to throw.
keep a sharp eye set on your target;
do not turn your back on your foe.
Real monsters lurk right on your
corner;
Goliath waits, wherever you go.

"My secrets cry aloud. I have no need
for tongue. My heart keeps open house,
my doors are widely swung. An epic of
the eyes my love, with no disguise…"
--- Theodore Roethke

MY THOUGHTS

My thoughts often go for a ride,
down almost any track;
and where they will go,
I cannot know;
but I cannot call them back.
My thoughts like carefree hobos,
hop the first train that comes
along;
with never a penny to pay their
fare; only a vagabond's song.
My thoughts are orphan children,
with no place to call home;
any open window or doorway,
is an invitation to roam.
My thoughts are shameless beggars,
on any road or street;
they boldly stick their hand out
for a hand out,
from anyone they chance to meet.
My thoughts are lonely travelers,
and never will they rest;
at each sunrise,
at each sunset;
they are off on their
endless quest.

ACHILLES THE POET

There was something of the poet
in Achilles, prompting him to
reject the gods bribe:
a long carefree life of anony-
mity,
to tempt his mortality.
Choosing instead a short life of
lasting fame,
to immortalize his name;
he staked out forever his claim
to Mt. Olympus.

"It takes surprise and wild connec-
tions… Words that never knew each
other till right now… Try untried
circuitry, new fuses…"
--- Edward Lueders

POEMS ARE PEOPLE

Poems are people with warm faces
that wear,
"We care",
becomingly.
Poems are people with young smiles
that beg,
"Lets play",
enthusiastically.
Poems are people with calloused
hands that plead,
"Come, let's go,
convincingly.
Poems are people with frank
words that say, "Listen",
compellingly.
Poems are people with searching
minds who inquire, "Shall we?",
invitingly.
Poems are people like you,
and people like me.

ATTENTION PLEASE

Attention please! This sound you
hear,
is just my poem, knocking on your
ear.
"May I come in? I've a message
for you fresh from my pen."
Listen please! This sound you
hear,
is only my verse tapping at your
ear.
"Let me come in. I've a song for
you,
fresh from my heart,
my song is new.
Attention please!

"Lay me on an anvil, O God,
Beat me and hammer me into a
crowbar. Let me pry loose old
walls. Let me lift and loosen
old foundations…"
--- Carl Sandburg

AH LIFE

Ah life!
It is but a spicy dash
of poetic nonsense, ala Oggie Nash.
And yet, 'tis also an idiot's tale;
a Shakespearean sonnet that has long
since grown stale.
Ah life:
It is naught but a chuckle or a sneer;
a romantic lay, as Lizzie Browning
just might say;
or else a lecherous limerick from
ole Edward Lear.
Ah life!
It is but a Homeric Odyssey:
an epic journey into tragedy;
yet still, one could say 'tis a
pot of witches brew;
a sorcerer's portion of
abracadabra stew.
Ah life:
you are but a poetpourri;
a poet's potion of confusing,
and amusing musery.

GIVE ME A POEM

Give me a poem
that will jump any wall,
and never take a fall.
Give me a poem
that will climb and never stop,
until it gains the mountain top.
Give me a poem
that will challenge any current,
brave any tide;
will swim any river,
no matter how wide.
Give me a high jumper.
Give me a swimmer.
Give me a mountain climber,
for a poem.

"Poetry is metaphor, saying one
thing and meaning another…"
--- Robert Frost

COLOR THIS POEM YOU

Color this poem young,
something green newly sprung
from some hidden songspring,
a becoming thing.
Color this poem new,
something bright a dream of blue
bathing in infant light.
Color this poem soft, something
light borne aloft on mornings"
breeze,
a lovesong of sky and trees.
Color this poem love,
something unseen; a perfect blend
of green and blue,
color this poem you.

YOU ARE POETRY

You are the poem I cannot
write,
lost in the darkness of the
night
that fills me;
trapped in the maze of
memory that haunts me;
you are poetry.
You are the song I cannot
sing,
the winter's welcoming of
spring
that has passed me;
locked in the nightingale's
throbbing throat,
you are melody.
You are the life I cannot
live,
buried in the breast of
earth
that more me;
a see of spirit tossed on
the breath of time;
conceived in the womb of
living,
you are love.

"...You start toward the unknown,
swimming in uncharted seas every
time you write a poem..."
--- Stanley Kunitz

NOAHS

We begin as Noah;
leaving our safe ark
we embark on our journey
over tempestuous seas,
one by one into the tempest we go!
We begin as David;
facing a scowling Goliath
armed with but sling and stone
we battle the mocking foe
naked and alone!
We begin as Daniel;
cast into the lion's den
our backs to the wall,
we take hold and wrestle the beast
until we fall!
We begin as Moses;
cast adrift on seas of chance
we ride the tide of circumstance,
and on the shores of an unknown land
we make our final stand!
"I cannot rest from travel; I will
drink life to the lees... For always
roaming with a hungry heart, much
have I seen and known... I am a part
of all that I have met... And this gray
spirit yearning in desire to follow
knowledge, like a sinking star, beyond
the utmost bound of human thought...

For my purpose holds to sail beyond the
sunset, and the baths of all the west-
ern stars until I die... Come, my
friends, 'tis not too late to seek a
newer world..."
--- Alfred L. Tennyson

"Give all to meaning. The free-
dom is ours to insist on mean-
ing..."
--- Robert Frost

POETICALLY YOURS

Dear Poets,
You who would take the world by the
tail, and give it one big swing;
you who would take the bull by
his horns, and grab for the
golden ring;
then be only yourself and no one
but yourself; if you would do
something do nothing but your own
thing.
You who would play the walrus
and make the world your pot of
oyster stew;
you who would put your hand to
the plow,
poetically I say to you:
be bold; take hold!
Go on and grab the world by
its' tail,
don't worry that you could fail;
go ahead, cook yourself your own
pot of oyster stew;
but be sure to reserve a place
at your table for this hungry poet,
please do.
Dear poets,
please listen to what I say
and take my advice today;
Go forth a knight in poet's armor,

find a fire breathing dragon to
slay.
If you cannot find your dragon,
look for a windmill on your way.
Be a true to life Don Quixote!
Go out and make this poet's day!

"Every poem is an epitome of the great
predicament; a figure of the will
braving alien entanglements…"
--- Robert Frost

POETRY IS METAPHOR

If you can believe Robert Frost
when he speaks of poetry;
and it would be hard to dismiss
such a master of the muse as he;
all there is to writing poetry
is one word, "metaphor";
it is just this simple,
that is all there is to it;
just metaphor--- and nothing
more.
but there is something more
with metaphor:
you change what is into what
could be;
you make the impossible very
possible,
the unreal becomes reality.
This then is the challenge
and the purpose of poetry:
to breathe life into the
non-living; to resurrect the dead;
to animate the inanimate,
to fleshen the spirit; from your
own brow, to harvest bread.
It is within the power of the pet,
to defy, not deify deity;
to confront, to confound;
to astound, not propound
immortality.
"Long live the weeds that overwhelm

my narrow vegetable realm!
All things unholy, marred by curse,
the ugly of the universe.
Hope, love, create, or drink and die:
these shape the creature that is I..."
--- Theodore Roethke

"Where is a poem?
As far away as a rainbow span,
ancient Cathay, or Afghanistan?

THE POEM AND I

I saw a poem walking, walking, walking,
I saw a poem walking,
when I took a walk today.
I heard a poem talking, talking, talking
I heard a poem talking,
here is what I heard it say:
"Let's you and I go singing,
go swinging, go winging;
let's you and I go singing,
it's such a lovely day!"
Then off we went together,
together, together;
the poem and I together,
our hearts so young and gay.
We stopped to say, "Good morning.
How are you this morning?"
We paused to say, "Good morning."
to boys and girls at play.
The children all came with us,
came laughing, came singing;
and all of us went dancing
on a skippy springy day.
We greeted the smiling sunrise,
waved back to friendly flowers;
sang along with birds and breezes,
in the cheery month of May.
On we went hopping, springing,
our hearts so full of music;
in bright and happy weather,

we went singing on our way.
Or it can be near as where
you stand this very day
on main Street here,
with a poem in your hand..."
--- Eve Merriam

"Be with me in the sacred
witchery of almostness…"
--- e.e. cummings

READ MY POEM

Read my poem, read me:
hear my voice speak to you;
I'll tell you who I am,
and just where I am.
In learning who I am,
in knowing where I am,
you too may discover just
who you are and where you are?
Read my poem, read me:
feel my thoughts commune with you.
My words will tell you just
what I think and why I think
as I do.
In learning what I think,
in knowing how I think,
quite possibly you will learn
what you think, and just why
you think as you do?
Read my poem, read me, know me:
read my poem, read yourself,
know yourself.
Read my poem, hear me, see me,
know me; read my poem, hear, see,
know yourself--- through my poetry.

STARSINGER

The poet felt the surgings
of a universe within,
and saw the heavens dance
at the tip of his pen.
He felt the fiber worn deep
with age,
and saw galaxies at play
on an empty page.
He heard the song that only
the heart can sing;
so each cold December dawn,
burst forth into spring!

"He dares to live who stops being a
bird yet beats his wings, against the
immense immeasurable emptiness of
things…"
---Theodore Roethke

POETRY IS LIFE

Poetry is a dirty faced
barefoot boy,
sticking his tongue out
at the mirror.
Poetry is a freckle faced
pigtailed girl,
making faces at
Old Miss Fuddyduddy.
Poetry is life,
thumbing its' nose at death;
shouting with its' very last
breath: "You big bully!"

POETRY

In the state of poetoria,
in a town named, Poetryville;
a lonely poem came knocking,
at a house on the muse's hill.
"May I please come in?"
The poet whispered.
"Oh yes, please do come in,"
a voice inside said.
So the poem very softly, stepped into
a welcome head.
"Please sit down," the host invited;
"I'll prepare us a pot of tea."
Then the poem, with his new friend
beside him, together shared their poetry.
"I am a poet", said the host, "and I
write poetry. Tell me my friend, what is
your name?"
"I am a poem," the guest replied quickly;
"and poetically speaking, poetry's the
name of my game."
So, the poet and the poem,
two good friends sat there;
just enjoying each other's company.
And as the night turned into day,
with their poetic word play,
they created their own poetry.

the hours descend,
putting on stars…
in the street of the sky night walks
scattering poems…"
e.e. cummings
"The figure a poem makes:
it begins in delight and ends in wisdom.
It ends in a clarification of life itself,
a momentary stay against confusion…"
--- Robert Frost

"The ordinary man lives by the
creative spirit. He thinks in
images and dreams in fantasy;
he lives by poetry..."
--- Louis Untermeyer

ONLY THE POET

Only the poet who lives inside
each of us, can see the smile
behind the tears;
the vision of the poet looks
ahead for the next ten thousand
years.
Only the poet who lives inside
each of us, hears the laughter
beneath the cry;
and listens to the silence that
speaks, in a weary sigh.
Only the poet who lives inside
each of us, speaks the language
of deity;
and can translate an immortal
tongue,
for mere mortality.

A POET LIFTS HIS PEN

A bird lifts it's wing,
preparing to fly;
then launches it's fragile
feathered craft,
upon an ocean of sky.
A poet lifts his pen,
preparing to write;
then sets sail upon
uncharted seas…
that invite! Excite! Incite!

"Like a piece of ice on a hot
stove the poem must ride on its'
own melting. A poem may be work-
ed over once it is in being, but
may not be worried into being…"
--- Robert Frost

POET 007

The poet is a very real
James Bond type,
a true to life 007;
he's at liberty to thrill,
with a license to kill;
and he will send you straight
to hell or to heaven.
His mission: to kill
bigotry and prejudice;
and their stooges ignorance,
fear and hate.
With his poetic golden gun,
he'll put these bad guys on
the run;
to hopefully save the earth
a tragic fate;
and rescue the human race,
before it's too late.
The poet has gone gunning
for the golden calves of greed;
and for the sacred cows of
Sodom, who feed their every
need.
He's off to kill the fatted
kine;
to hunt down over Bo-Peep
who is leading his sheep

to the sacrificial altar;
to gun down the chic sleek
swine:
the all-of-one-kind, all-of-
one-mind; blind-who-lead-the-
blind to their slaughter.

"Silence beyond the mystery of rhyme…
--- e.e. cummings

THIS POEM

This poem
is for whoever has the light out
and can't see in the dark…
All too often would-be-poets
are too busy turning out the
light on someone groping
in the darkness…
Obviously there were not many
masters of the muse on hand
when the Great Poet lifted
His hand to write:
"Let there be light…"
Still lurking in the shadows
were pretenders at the art,
beguiling the naïve;
enter Adam, enter Eve…
Of for a poet who can throw
some light on a thing or two,
and has the will too…

PRICKUPINE

This poem is a prickupine
to stick the soft behind;
to prick the comfy rear,
to twist the tone deaf ear.
This poem is a stickupine
to stir the sleepy mind;
to puncture the peaceful content,
to disrupt the safe intent.
This poem is a pokeupine
to rouse the coddled secure
from their shelter
labeled safe,
from their path marked
so sure.

"Piper sit thee down and write
in a book that all may read---
and I made a rural pen, and I
stain'd the water clear,
and I wrote my happy songs
every child may joy to hear..."
--- William Blake

I AM A POEM

I am a poem:
I am always hungry for
something good to eat;
just what should a poem eat?
On what special treat,
what prime meat can I feed,
to meet a poem's need?
I am a poem:
I am forever thirsty for
some refreshing drink;
just what should a poem drink,
do you think?
What special beverage will
quench my thirst?
Just what should I try first?

HOW TO TASTE A POEM

Take one small slice and lift it
slowly to your mouth;
wrap it around your tongue, and
then,
let your teeth sink in.
A little salt, pepper, spice;
some sugar, vinegar, herbs,
that should suffice.
Don't let the flavor
slip away, to savor,
chew ever so slow, not too fast;
let the rhythm linger;
let the poetry last.

A POEM COMING ON

I feel a poem coming on:
someone's tapping in my head,
"Let me out! I want to shout
loud enough for all to hear;
I have a message for some
special ear.
Please open wide and let me
step outside!"
Somebody's pounding on my brain,
"Set me free! Unlock this prison
door; remove my chains,
I want to proclaim liberty.
To everyone who is captive,
down with slavery!
Someone is knocking on my heart,
"May I come in?
I have something unique to give;
but I must be born so I can live.
I bring a wing for some fledgling
bird;
I sing a song that has never been
heard.
Please open your heart, my friend!

THE RAIN POET

Tiny orbs, you charm the skies
of those celestial bodies far;
in your mirrored reflection lies,
the inner bliss of soft lullabies
from a distant star.
Blessed the hand that formed
your soul,
to cleanse, to refresh
all life here below;
you add your fleshening power
to both high and low.
Valleys of green,
fields of brown--- drink!
With open arms their besoms
yield,
to echo your praise in song.

The Sharpest Sword

Words can be sharper
than the sharpest sword,
they can slay a savage monster,
they can stop a marauding horde...
Words can be colder
than the coldest steel,
they can make the coward bolder,
force the mightiest man to kneel...
Words can be hotter
than the hottest fire,
they can stir the ire of passion,
fan the hot flames of desire...
Words can be harder
than the hardest stone,
they can fell a giant Goliath,
kill an army with a bone...
Words can be softer
than a feather's touch,
gentler than a baby's skin,
calmer than the dawn's shy blush...
Words can be duller
than the dullest knife,
they can cut the joy from living,
gnaw the happiness out of life...
Words can be faster
than the fastest gun,
they can rescue all the "good guys,"
put the "bad guys" on the run...
Words can be slower
than a turtle or a snail,
they run just like molasses,
they come like Christmas mail.....

THE OLD POET

The old poet poetically, cast a
poetical eye;
at a pile of trash, a clump of weeds,
and a flowering rosebush nearby.
Then the old poet, poetically,
on that very poetical day;
bemused himself, being himself a
muse, by penning this poetical lay:
As surely as the heavens cover the
earth; as surely as the evening
follows the morn;
he who sleeps in a bed of roses,
must himself wear a crown of thorn!

I THE POEM SAY

I the poem say, "Look at me.
Just words on paper;
is this all that you see?
Behind each word that is chosen
with so much care,
look close and you may see someone
waiting for you there.
You may see a master chef cooking up
his gourmet recipe?
Or an angler casting out his line,
if you look real close, you just may see."
I the poem say, "Look closely at me.
Just lines on a page,
is this all that you can see?
Now look very carefully, for behind
any line;
you may find someone who is looking
for you at almost any time.
Could it be a fisherman who is baiting
his hook;
hoping to reel in a big fish with a
good line from his book?
Close your eyes now and make a wish.
Do you think that you might be this fish?
Once the poet catches you on his hook,
you may find that you are one for the
fisherman's book.
And who knows, on some far off future day,
you may just be the Big One, who did not
get away?"
I the poem say, "Take a much closer look
at me.
Just a verse in a book; is this all that

you really do see?
Look again now, but much much closer;
and listen carefully, oh yes please do.
Can you hear those far away places
that are calling just to you?
From exotic Baghdad to ancient Timbuktu;
hear them call, "Come! Will you please
come? Do you hear me calling you?'
I the poem now ask you, Shall we go now,
just me and you?"

A POET IS HIS NAME

A poet is his name,
and he's gone hunting for big game.
He's hunting the ravenous wolves that
are stalking the helpless fold;
those wild beasts of prey that lust only
for green gold.
The poet is his name,
and he is out for big game.
He is looking for wild animals of insatiable
bloodlust;
and ferreting out these killer rogues is
the poet's sacred trust.
And he won't rest for he cannot rest,
until the last one bites the dust.
A poet is his name,
and he is stalking big game.
He is searching for wild jackals
that prey on the weak;
hungry hyenas that stalk the helpless;
wild dogs grown fat and sleek.
These are the slimy sewer rats that
any real poet must seek.
The poet is his name,
and bagging varmints is his game.
He's sniffing out the stinky polecats
who pollute the air;
and he is going to track those smelly skunks,
straight to their own plush lair.
A poet is his name,
and he's aiming to slush out foul game.
He is hunting for the old buzzards,
who roost away up high;
and these vile vultures from their nests,

are keeping a watchful eye.
They know the poet is out for foul prey,
and they are spreading their wings to fly.
The poet is his name,
and he's gone hunting slick game.
He is tracking down all creepy things,
every slippery snake-in-the-grass;
each slimy eel with that banana peel feel;
every wiggly worm, he will make them
all squirm. The Poet won't let anything pass.

"Poetry provides not merely an ex-
perience but the significance of an
experience; not merely a wild wind but
a feeling for the mystery in the sound
of wind at night…"
--- May Arbuthnot

A BONE TO PICK

You poets,
you prince and princess of the pen;
you who would dare to speak to
that still small voice in men;
I have a bone to pick with you:
if you would touch a stranger's
heart in some distant unknown
land,
then walk right next door and
shake you neighbor's hand.
You poets,
you master and mistress of the muse
how can you plant hope in some
barren heart,
when there is no dream blooming
within your own breast?
How can your hands harvest the
sweet fruit of hope,
when you've abandoned your own
dream quest?
You poets,
you guardians of hope, you keep-
ers of dreams:
how do you lead another through
the dark terrain of night,
with eyes that have lost their
sight?

How can you give someone your
very best,
when your soul thinks only of
comfort and rest?
To dream and see; to reach and
touch, is to hold heaven and
earth in your hand;
to feel, to grasp, to nurture
hope; is to rule both sky
and land.

"The poet goes back and forth over the
same territory as other men in their
day to day occupations, in their strug-
gle for survival, in their delight and
dismay at life. But he sees more and he
tells more; he takes us to far-off places
we have seen only in dreams or to nearby
places we have visited but, in the deep-
est sense, never reached…"
--- William Jay Smith

THE PANHANDLER POET

A poem goes tap-tapping
down a one-way dead-end street;
a poor Lazarus begging bread,
seeking shoes for his barren feet.
A poet goes panhandling for a
magical metaphor;
searching for a savory simile,
pleading, "Please give me one more."
A poem is a panhandler,
its' hand is always out;
looking for one crumb of meaning
that might be lying about.
The poet is a poor panhandler,
his hungry mind always reaching for:
just one small slice of simile;
a mere morsel of metaphor.

MAN: A POEM?

Man, unpenned line of poetry;
unwritten verse of the universe;
unsung song called humanity.
Man, strong as simile, like a rhyme;
without a reason and out of season.
Without a rhyme,
out of place and out of time.
Man, oh mighty metaphor;
majestic mountain high;
flashing crashing meteor,
lighting up the sky.
A ravenous raging river,
a deep ocean wide;
a dry and lifeless desert
where snake and scorpion hide.

16 LINES OR LESS

According to Mr. Frost,
a man seldom lost
for a good poetic word;
it is better left unwritten
and unheard,
any ill conceived line of poetry.
If any prince or princess of the pen,
can't say what nees to be said
in 16 lines or less,
better to leave that thought unsaid;
it is best to leave that poem dead.
Any master of the muse
can ill afford to abuse
his or her power of the pen;
that's the poet's unpardonable sin.
Amen!

DON'T THINK

When you challenge the status
quo,
things as they are,
don't think that the starmakers
whoever they may be,
will award you a gold star.
When you question what is,
and criticize what will be,
don't think the powers that be,
whoever they might be,
will invite you in for tea.
When you put down business as
usual,
the traditional acceptable way;
when the sacred cows
of the One Of Us Club,
you attempt to slay;
don't think these cowboys
will say to you:
"Hey good buddy. Do you have a
nice day."
"Poetry is a smiling face,
that bends your frowns
upside down…"
---Elizabeth Horne

Dear poets,
please listen to what I say
and take my advice today:
Go forth a knight in poet's armor,
find a fire breathing dragon to
slay.
If you cannot find your dragon,
look for a windmill on your way.
Be a true to life Don Quixote!
G out and make this poet's day!

HOW DO YOU POET?

How do you poet?
Take a small seed from the poetree;
sow it, till it, tend it.
How do you rhyme?
Take childish feet,
teach them your beat,
then how to tell time.
How do you muse?
Learn when to use and to refuse;
how to amuse yet not abuse.

KHAYAM RHYAM

A slice of bread and a glass of wine
perhaps a cute angle; a curvaceous
line;
and who knows, this old Khayam,
just might compose a rhyam?
Poems
are vehicles
that run on word power;
they carry idea
for their cargo.

"By daying daily, I have come
to be…"
--- Theodore Roethke

OF POETS AND KINGS

The poet and the king sat down to dine;
the king proposed a toast,
lifting his golden goblet of wine:
"I drink to someone, this is no boast,
one who is ruler of all the world,
and of all things the very most
powerful creature upon the face of
this earth;
I give you now your royal host…"
the poet raised his well worn pen,
and in measured response to the king
he did begin:
"Great King!
Although your might and power may
rule both sea and land,
I hold even a greater power right
here in the palm of my hand:
a power that moves only at my bidding,
that obeys only the poet's command.
For down through all the ages past,
throughout the vast volumes of time;
every army that ever marched,
every monarch who ever ruled,
has been subject to the poet's rhyme.
For the master of the muse,
with such power may refuse
even a crown or a kingdom to a king;
and among this race called men,
only the poet's pen,
may teach even a mute how to sing.

Oh yes, oh mighty king,
there is a power far greater
than the king's crown and sword.
Before the power of the poet's pen,
even royalty must bend;
for the pen is much mightier
than the sword!
The pen of the poet, Great King
is Lord!"

"One day I felt a mountain touch me
where I stood… A valley spilled
its tickling river in my eyes…"
--- e.e. cummings

RIDE 'EM COWBOY

Hey there! All you poets!
Be a rootin' tootin',
sonofagun square shootin'
real he-man John Wayne today.
Ride out on the range and round
up a lonely stray;
or rustle up a sacred cow or two
on your way
Lasso those fat cows, and put
your brand on 'em too;
then butcher a couple and cook
up a big pot of that good ole
sacred cow stew.
Hey there! All you poets!
Be an outlaw, a Billy The Kid.
Add a notch or two to your
trusty poetry gun;
put those no good bush-whackin'
dirty varmints on the run.
Those rustlin' coyotes,
those sidewinders and polecats
need to pay;
so, go out and ride 'em cowboy!
Ride out and make a poet's day!

DUES BLUES

While the Great Poet up above
is taking Himself a snooze,
we poets,
His children down here below,
are singing the blues
as we pay our dues.
So I ask you now,
just what else is news?

"The object in writing poetry is
to make all poems sound as dif-
ferent as possible from each
other…"
--- Robert Frost

POETIQUETTE

How do you address a poem,
as Ms. or Mrs. Mr. or Sir?
Or should it be he or she;
they or them; him or her?
When you meet an elfish limerick
and he teases you:
"Bet you can't catch me!"
Do you play the monkey and
chase the weasel,
all around the mulberry tree?
should you greet a stylish
sonnet, who is so very proper
and prim;
do you doff your hat and curtsey?
Do you ask, "How about a swim?"
When west meets east in haiku,
do you ask: "Hi! How are you?"
Perhaps you invitingly query,
"Tea for two?"
And then before tomorrow,
it could be sayonara?
When you invite a poem to eat,
it is perfectly poetical to
serve a poetreat.
When you sit down with a poem
to dine,

it is proper poetiquette to
to offer for a toast,
a vintage poetical line.
"Be you clown or be you king,
still your singing is the
thing…"
--- Laura E. Richards

"From whence cometh song?
From the tear far away,
from the hound giving tongue,
from the quarry's weak cry?..."
--- Theodore Roethke

POETRY

I think that I will never see,
a thing as fair as poetry.
A poem that may so joyfully bring,
gifts of warmest welcoming.
A poem that may laugh, and dance,
and sing;
in summer, fall, winter, spring.
A poem whose open arms may share,
with someone its' heartfelt care.
Upon whose time lined face is worn,
the sweat and tears of thoughts
unborn.
Whose heart beats to the rhythms of
a universal song of love.

PARLOR PET POETS

You jingle jugglers,
you dope smugglers,
selling your Madison Avenue line:
"Here's to ya! A little dab'll do!
Things go better with coke!"
Some sick joke.
Conning unsuspecting folk.
Today's featured attraction:
Lights! Camera! Action!
For the little old ladies of
Park Avenue,
a tasty tidbit for chic chicks
to chew,
from their fast food menu.
You call yourself poet?
You're nothing but
Park Avenue's parlor pet;
an after dinner drink
for every nerd and fink
of the Madison Avenue jet set.

"Let me have men about me that
are fat. Yon Cassius has that
lean and hungry look. He thinks
too much. Such men are dangerous…"
--- William Shakespeare

WANTED DEAD OR ALIVE, A POET:

Wanted dead or alive, A. Poet:
he is well armed and very danger-
ous too.
Keep a sharp eye out,
when the poet is about,
lest he draw a bead on you.
Which is just what a good poet will do.
Wanted dead or alive, A. Poet:
he may be found rounding up a sacred
cow or two.
First he ropes them, then he butchers
them; then he throws them in a pot.
And then he cooks up a batch of
delicious sacred cow stew.
Now that is something that a real
poet would do.
Wanted dead or alive, A. Poet:
this outlaw a true to life real
Robin Hood.
Chasing the bad guys in his black hat,
he's a good guy, imagine that.
This square shooting punslinger
has an itchy trigger finger;
with his deadly poet's gun,
he's Billy the Kid and Jesse James
all in one.

Wanted dead or alive, A. Poet:
he is the most dangerous man
in the entire world today.
He insists on being himself,
thinking for himself;
and in having his own say,
and living his own life,
in his--- and only his own way.

"Poets stick to nothing deliberately,
but let what will stick to them like
burrs where they walk in the fields…"
--- Robert Frost

COCKLEBURR

this poem is a cocklebur,
to stick under the saddle
of he who sits astraddle
the well groomed steed of
success.
To pick the pampered pride of
he who seeks to ride the
well fed thoroughbred of
power.
Of he who would be crowned
the chosen Man of The Hour.
Let it be a thorn in the side.
Let it spur the sleek hide.
Let it burrow beneath soft
skin.
Let it dig in.
Let it stick.
Let it ride.

PIG POET

Oh brother mine,
my fellow swine;
we share a common lot:
this plot
of muck and mire;
this pigpen our funeral
pyre.
Feet sinking knee deep
in slime,
catch the slippery essence
of rhyme;
tongue tasting pungent slop
savors the subtle simile in
each drop.
Oh prodigal poet, this your
role: root out some solid
metaphor in this mudhole."

he word poet carries the
aroma of magic... To me poetry
is what is memorable... Poetry
turns up in unexpected places,
in unguarded moments..."
--- E.B. White

SORCERERS' STEW

The sorcerer adds his seasoning,
pouring a little reasoning
into his rhyme;
mixing in just one pinch more
of his meaty metaphor;
readying his vintage wine to pour.
Stirring in some savory simile,
he cooks up his gourmet recipe;
a potent potion of bewitching brew,
his poetic sorcerers' stew.
To his poet he adds one hens' tooth
so very rare;
a mythical haystack needle;
from the slippery wish fish one scale;
from the elusive sleep sheep
one hair from the tail.
You can see him on a moonlit night,
sowing his magic moonseed;
harvesting golden grapes of light
hanging heavy on the vine;
while a world thirsts for just one
taste of his sweet moonwine.
Then the sorcerer dons his
magicians' hat,
and just as a matter of habit
reaches in for a rabbit.
Suddenly, out of thin air,

alakazam! Abracadabra!"
A fluffy squirmy hare.
The sorcerer grows quite euphoric
when he waxes metaphoric;
creating a rhythmical fantasy,
with metaphorical musery!

"Freedom is nothing but departure,
setting forth, leaving things behind,
brave origination of the courage to be
new…"
--- Robert Frost

THE POET IN ME

It is the poet in me
who struggles to shed the yoke
of inevitability;
and free us all from the shackles
of mortality.
It is the poet in me
who wars against probability,
fighting for a real possibility;
what is, the way things are
is the poet's worst enemy.
It is the poet in me
who attacks the cancer of
conformity;
who defends the right to be free
to be me;
to object, to oppose, to confront,
to disagree;
to defend
my right to offend,
until the very end.
It is the poet in me
who daily wrestles deity;
who strains at these chains
enslaving all humanity;
who would free the human race,
the poet and poetry,
from all tyranny.
It is the poet in me

who jousts with windmills
continuously;
brandishing my sharp pensword as
off I go,
a would be Don Quixote,
fencing with the alien foe.

"The happenings of everyday life
are lifted out of the common-
place by the small, perfect frame
of words that poetry gives them."
--- May Arbuthnot

POETS WILL BE POETS

Boys will be boys, they say:
giving chase to each balloon
that chances to blow by;
a slight hint of mischief
in each boyish eye.
And then...
reaching in their pocket
with a devilish grin,
they pull out their pin
and stick it in!
Boys are boys, it's their way.
And poets will be poets,
sometimes anyway.
Boys will be boys, they say:
chasing little Miss Prissy
around and around the house;
sneaking up behind,
Surprise! A mouse!
And then...
EEEEEeeeeekkkkkKKKKK!!!!!
Boys are boys, it's their way.
And poets will be poets,
somehow someday.
Boys will be boys, they say:
doing handstands,
ala Bozo the Clown;
turning cartwheels and
hanging upside down.
boys are boys, it's their way.

And poets will be poets,
somewhere someway.
Boys will be boys, they say:
pulling a frog from a pocket;
flying a kite, firing a rocket.
Pulling a rabbit out of a hat;
did you see that?
Boys are boys, it's their way.
And poets will be poets,
anytime now, anyday.

YOUNG POETS OLD POETS

Young poets dream,
and old poets tell tales…
Young poets dream of:
mountains to climb,
rivers to cross;
ladies to woo,
foes to conquer,
and battles to win.
Old poets tell tales of:
mountains they have climbed,
rivers they have crossed;
ladies they have courted,
foes they have conquered,
and battles they have won.
But the mountains tell no stories
of those who have gained their
summit;
the rivers do not speak of who
may have crossed them;
ladies shy away from reveal-
ing their lovers;
foes rarely ever salute
their conquerors;
and battles lie mute
in the silence of death.
Still, young poets dream,
while old poets tell tales…..
"Never the murdered finalities of
yesno, impotent nongames of wrong
right and rightwrong; never to
gain or pause, never the soft ad-

venture of greedy anguishes and
cringing ecstasies of inexistence;
never to rest and never to have:
only to grow. Always the beautiful
answer who asks a more beautiful
question…"
--- e.e. cummings

Once one has learned to exper-
ience the poem as a poem, there
inevitably arrives the sense
that one is also experiencing
himself as a human being..."
--- John Ciardi

A POEM IS A PRETTY WOMAN

A poem is a pretty woman,
a melodic symphony;
a classic rhythmical composi-
tion,
a sonnet of symmetric rhapsody.
She's a seductress seducing,
enticing, with her poetic
harmony.
A poem is a pretty woman,
a flirtatious temptress coaxing,
"Come along!"
Romancing her excited lovers,
with her sultry siren song.
A poem is a pretty woman,
good measurements tempting and
teasing;
artistic treasure
for giving much pleasure;
and oh so very pleasing.
A poem is a pretty woman,
a well sculpted figure,
a masterpiece so fine;
beautiful body and face,
full of such style and grace;
shapely stanzas revealing her
form with rhythmic line.
"Who walks with beauty has no

need of fear; the sun and
moon and stars keep pace with
him... Who takes of beauty
wine and daily bread, will
know no lack when bitter
years are lean...
--- David Morton

"The person who gets close to poetry
is going to know more about the word
belief than anybody else…"
--- Robert Frost

WHEN THE GREAT POET
OF THE AGES

When the Great Poet of the ages
writes of me upon His pages,
I hope He can write enough to
make some rhyme and a bit of
reason,
out of my short season
of time upon lifes ever changing
stages.
When the Great Master of the Muse
sits down to write my name;
I don't ask for a place in
Heaven's Hall of Fame,
nor any place among the sages;
just one short line
on one of the Great Poet's pages,
would do just fine.
To make some sense
out of all this nonsense,
would be adequate recompense.
To create a short verse
from all of this adverse;
that would be much more a bless-
ing than a curse.

A POET---KNOW IT!

Hey there brother,
I am a poet,
and you had darn well better know it;
my ever sharp pen,
is posed and ready to do you in.
If you are a phony and full of
baloney, to the poet this is an
unpardonable sin.
yeah brother,
I am a poet;
and as sure as shootin',
you oughtta know it.

"Gather out of star-dust and
splinters of hail, one handful
of dream-dust not for sale…"
--- Langston Hughes

NOT ALL POEMS

Not all poems are symmetrical
sonnets,
penned by little old ladies
in pretty pink bonnets.
Not all poems are soft and
romantic,
mushy and gushy, no
some are very frantic!
Not each poem is a lyrical lay,
written by someone so happy,
so merry and so gay.
Not every poem is a lilting
rhyme,
authored by a poet just passing
his time.
No! N-O!
Some poems are sad,
and some are very mad.
Some are penned by a poet
just having his say;
others are written by someone
who is seeking his way.
Some poems are composed by poets
who have a game to play;
and others by those who just love
to play at word play.

THE WRESTLER

The poet
wrestles with angels,
he grapples with the air.
Like a Jacob,
he grabs the gods by the hair,
and will not let go,
until he delivers a
mortal blow.

"Hold fast to dreams, for if
dreams die, life is a broken
winged bird that cannot fly..."
--- Langston Hughes

DREAM BREAKERS

The world takes its' dreamers,
breaks them
and then makes them
ready for the mould it has cast.
It clips their wings,
locks them in a cage,
then it throws away the key;
no more precious freedom,
no more sweet liberty.
Locked in its' cage with
clipped wing,
a bird cannot fly yet being a
bird, it still can sing;
and defiantly beat its' wing
against the inevitability of
things.
And true to the nature of a
winged thing,
it can still sing the song only
a dreamer sings:
of open doors and open skies,
a welcome expanse for wings.

A POET'S WISH

To sow dreamseed in a hungry heart,
and watch them take root;
then cultivate them until they bear
delicious ripe dreamfruit.
To plant hopeshoots in fertile minds
tend them, watching them grow;
until they bear a poet of gold,
at the end of a magic rainbow.
To scatter poems in an empty life,
weeding and pruning regularly;
until they sprout, grow, and bloom
into a full grown living poetree.
"The world goes forth to murder
dreams..." --- e.e. cummings

"What happens to a dream de-
ferred? Does it dry up like a
raisin in the sun? Or fester
like a sore and then run?...
Maybe it just sags like a
heavy load? Or does it
explode?..."
--- Langston Hughes

ALIEN TO THE POET

To the poet,
Nothing dead or aalive,
nothing animate or inanimate;
nothing real or unreal,
nothing odd or strange;
nothing weird or different,
nothing concrete or abstract;
nothing one can smell or taste,
nothing one can see or hear;
nothing one can think or know---
is alien to the poet.
Not even what divides and
separates;
not necessarily that which tears
down and destroys;
not to stop, to abort, not even
to kill--- is alien to the poet.
Only that which destroys but
does not build; only that which
aborts and does not create;
only that which kills but cannot
hope or dream or grow.
Only this is alien to the poet:
only that which prevents humanity
from achieving its' highest possi-
bility.

Only that which prevents each human being from living a life worthy of the best in each human being--- the very best in each of us. Only what appeals to the least in each of us; to the worst in each of us--- only this is alien to the poet.

"We must be very gentle of our dreamers…"
--- Robert Frost

OH WORLD BE KIND

Oh world be kind to your dreamers.
Touch them with a gentle hand.
For they chart the course
and they set the sail,
for a far away unexplored land.
Oh world be good to your lovers.
Invite the into your heart.
For their moonlight lovesongs
and their sunrise serenade,
give each day a fresh
springlove start.
Oh world give heed to your poets.
Listen to them with attentive ear.
Their words that spring from a
fertile heartsoil,
cultivates hope;
and weeds out fear.

A POETREE

To
grow
poems;
give
affection;
cultivate with
your thought and mind;
give it your heart and soul.
Feed it with care it will root;
nurture it with plenty of time.
You plant a small seed in fertile soil:
A poetree,
poetry;
poet-
ry.

"It comes pretty hard on poetry,
I think what it has to bear in
the teaching process..."
--- Robert Frost

DOUBLE FROSTIC

The poet speaks of two roads parting,
and how he could not take them both
at the same time;
and for stating this thought in
verse, he was declared to be a
master of rhyme.
He said that there was something in
a wall that divided us, and made him
rebel;
but, then again, good fences do make
good neighbors, you know--- oh well.
So, he was hailed as a true prince
of the pen,
for posing this provocative dilemma
to men.
He labeled himself a swinger of
birches,
and said that "one could do worse";
and for making this observation
poetically,
he was described as an artisan of
verse.
He promised:
"But I have promises to keep..."
You politicians, whey you read this
line, fall down upon your knees and
weep!

THE POETS' PEN

The pen of the poet pricks comfortable
behinds, "Get up!"
Prods sleepy minds, "Wake up!"
He pokes lazy derrieres, "Bottoms up!"
And his pen tickles deaf ears,
"Open up!"

"Out of these nothings,
all beginnings come…"
--- e.e. cummings

A FUNNY THING

A funny thing happened
on the way to this poem:
the poet just lost his way,
like a lot of poets today.
He didn't quite know
just which way to go,
or quite what to say.
When you are not too sure
which way you should go,
just dig out a coin and
give it a throw.
Heads you lose,
and tails you lose;
sounds just like that same
old news losers' blues.
Which way? Who cares anyway?
All roads lead to the same
deadend, sometime,
somewhere, someday.
You don't know quite
what to say?
You cop a plea:
Well now, you see…
If every dog must have
his day,
then every poet will have
his say---
somehow.
someway,
someday.

"Poetry knows no bounds.
Nobody can tell you exactly
what poetry is or isn't…"
--- Richard Peck

SLINGSHOT POET

David the poet,
the warrior,
like any man knew fear;
still he cast off the stiff armor
of tradition,
took his sling and his stone
in his hand,
and bravely went forth
to save his land.
David the poet,
the dreamer,
looked up at the stars above;
and he heard the firmament singing
heaven's symphony of love.
And a song stirred within David's
breast,
giving him the courage to meet this
test.
David the poet,
the shepherd,
he saw the hills dancing,
and heard the mountains singing
their song.
And so David, the shepherd boy,
feeling their joy,
danced and sang along.
David the poet,
was a man set apart;
with his songs David,
sweet singer of Israel,
captured God's own heart!

THE POET A DAVID

The poet, a modern day David,
armed with but a sling and a stone;
goes forth to face the Goliaths of
ignorance and despair;
to battle these legions of half truth,
and untruth;
without conjuring up a single "Thus
saith" or "forsooth."
Without even pronouncing a final, "Amen,"
He turns them all aside with one thrust
of his mighty pen.
The poet, a real live David,
and a man who is set apart;
strides out to face the wild beasts alone;
a man after God's own heart.
His eyes look at the world afresh,
with wondrous imaginings.
He dances with the dancing hills;
and he flies on eagle's wings.

BE POETS

You poets,
don't cast your poetic pearls
to the feet of swine;
sharpen your poetic pen,
polish your poetic line.
You are off to slay the
fatted kine,
those golden calves of Babylon;
let the rabble babble on!
You poets,
why drink the slop and eat the
husks of the pigpen?
Get up off your knees, stand on
your own two feet and be men.
Pick up your sword,
claim your just reward:
the fat pigs of whoredom;
the silken whores of Sodom.
You poets,
you prodigal sons,
come on out of your pigpen;
Stand up! On guard! Present arms!
Be poets--- be men!

TO COOK UP A POEM

To cook up a poem,
let it simmer s-l-o-w-l-y;
add a pinch of simile to taste;
pour in a touch of metaphor
to season;
then add just enough rhyme
to fit your reason.
Set it on the back burner and
let it simmer s-l-o-w-l-y for
some time;
turn it over at least once or twice
in your mind;
be aware of the time;
be very careful with the rhyme.
Remember to tend your poem well,
seasoning it quite liberally;
you'll cook up a gourmet recipe,
a tasty treat of appetizing
poetpourri to eat.

TO WRITE A NEW POEM

The way to write a new poem;
something that no one else has written,
something that no one has ever said;
something that has never lived until now,
and until now has been dead?
You plant a small seed of a fresh idea
in someone's fertile head.
You introduce new words to new thoughts;
give them some time to know each other well.
Who knows, before very long, they may have
an interesting story to tell?
Let them share their tales of home
and far away places;
a little laughter, a good cry;
and some memorable faces.
Let them remember many things they have
done together;
the varied experiences they have shared
in both fair or foul weather.
After the words and thoughts have visited
for a time,
just give them a pen and some paper.
They just may compose a rhyme?

"Miracles are to come. With you
I leave a remembrance of mir-
acles; they are by somebody who
can love and who will be contin-
ually reborn…"
--- e.e. cummings

WHO WOULD BE POET

Who would be poet let him not
turn his back on the wind
but face to face,
let him meet the wrath
that he may know his place,
may find his path.
Who would be poet let him not
hide his face from the sun
but eye to eye,
let him face the hungry fire
that he may feel
the hot desire.
Who would be poet let him not
cover his head form the rain;
let him embrace the chill,
that he may know the pain,
may feel the thrill.
Who would be poet let him not
shun the heat,
shut out the cold;
let him throw open his arms
to all things young,
to all things old.
Who would be poet,
let him welcome both winter
and spring,
if he would give a word its' wing;
if he would teach a bird to sing.

"Let your verse be a winged
living thing fleeing, we feel,
from a soul in flight towards
other skies, other loves…"
--- Paul Verlaine

IT PAYS TO BE A POET

It pays to be a poet Noah,
when casting off in your fragile ark;
should you be Lot's wife
from Sodom and Gomorrah,
get ready to say your, "Sayonnara!"
It pays to be the poet Moses,
if you are set adrift,
cast out on the deep;
if you should perhaps be Pharoah,
prepare yourself to weep.
It pays to be a poet David,
when facing a Goliath alone;
if you are King Saul,
you may stand tall,
but you'll need more than sling
and stone.
It pays to be the poet Jacob,
when wrestling angels unaware;
if not, it would be best for you
to catch the devil by his hair.
It pays to be a poet Daniel,
when cast into the lion's den;
if a doubting Thomas you happen
to be, prepare to say, "Amen!"
It pays to be the poet Jonah,
when you are swallowed by a whale;
if you are just a little fish,
your story will likely end
as one more tall fishing tale.

"Let your verse be sheet good
luck scattered in the crisp
gusts of morning wind that
arrive breathing mint and
thyme…"
--- Paul Verlaine

"because you are forever making poems
in the lap of death Humanity I hate
you…"
--- e.e. cummings

SO MANY POETS

So many poets are pet pussycats
licking their masters' dirty hands,
peacefully purring pets sitting
in the lap of power;
meowing at every, "Here,
kitty, kitty, kitty, kitty!'
Now how about an itty bitty ditty?
Oh for a wild alley cat,
an old tomcat, prowling the dark-
ness for a big fat sewer rat.
So many poets are tame lapdogs,
gnawing on the bones their
masters throw;
licking the smelly feet of success;
barking at their own shadow.
Chasing their own tail,
fetching a stock at every,
"Fetch boy! Go fetch! Go!"
Bones and sticks, some tricks!
Oh for a lean mean old bloodhound,
a mangy old mongrel cur,
who recognizes no master.
So many poets are caged birds
with clipped wings;
they have no new songs to sing,
but only a few stale parrotings
to whoever coaxes, "Polly want a
cracker?"
Hey there now Polly Parrot,
how would you like a carrot?

YUK

Frankie on poetry,
frankly speaking:
"Poetry?
Yuk!"

"Ah when to the heart of man was it
ever less than treason, to go with
the drift of things, to yield with a
grace to reason, and bow and accept
the end of a love or a season..."
--- Robert Frost

ACCEPTANCE

To the poet the word "acceptance",
is an unacceptable 4-letter word;
that same old go along just to
get along song,
oh so many many times, too many
he has heard.
For it is not in the nature of
the poet to go along,
just to get along;
to him it's not enough just to
belong.
If you want him to dance, then
sing another song.
Just to always go with the way
things are, may have a strong
appeal to reason;
but to any poet who is worthy of
the name, this is the highest
form of treason.
To just ride with the tide, and
never rock the boat;
just to keep the frail craft
safely afloat,
to the poet this thinking
strikes a sour note.
Just to go with the flow,
and roll with the punch;

holy bazooka, you wannabe Palooka!
Know it, to the poet,
you re out to lunch.
To bow and to bend
to the whim of every wind,
to the poet worth his salt,
and to all of poetry;
this is an unpardonable sin,
and the utmost blasphemy!

"All there is to writing is having
ideas. To learn to write is to learn
to have ideas…"
--- Robert Frost

WHEN A POET WRITES

When a poet writes he doesn't
write with one eye fixed on the
Pulitzer Prize, the other just
matter of factly on what he is
writing;
he hangs no: "For Sale" sign out
his window, and answers to no ads:
"For Hire", inviting.
A poet does not write to create
after dinner conversation for the
Country Club Set;
none of this chic "with it"
mumbo jumbo;
he's no lapdog to be led on his
leash, he's nobody's dumbo.
He's not blind;
he doesn't just rub some
well scrubbed behind.
A poet does not write to become
the keynote applause meter for
some well polished politico, no.
No comfy coddled soul he;
no party animal--- no siree!
The poet does not tickle a ten-
der ear;
he may have to clean out the wax,
so it can hear.
And you had darn well better
well know it:
he is a poet.

POET SAY

Poet say:
if poet not watch,
where poet put foot,
poet may step in something.

A POET'S REQUEST

Let me be the fly,
spoiling Miss Sweetie Pie's
piece of pie;
Let me be the flea,
ruining old Mr. Fuddy Duddy's
cup of tea.
Let me be the bug,
crawling underneath Mr. Bigwig's
rug;
Let me be the pin,
pricking Miss Pretty Thing's
perfumed skin.
Let me be the air,
mussing up Mr. Debonair's well
groomed hair;
Let me be the ants,
biting in Miss Persnickety's
new pants.
Let me be the rock,
scratching in Mr. High Stocking's
soft silk sock;
Let me be the bee,
stinging Miss Sugar Plum's sweet
as honey knee.
Let me be the glue,
gumming up Mr. Bootlicker's
polished shoe;
Let me be the rub,
in Old Miss Spick And Span's
shiney brand new tub.
Let me be the thorn,
sticking in Miss Lovey Dovey's
rosey morn;

let me be the spear,
spearing Mr. Comfortable's
coddled rear.
Let me be the burr,
burrowing beneath Miss Dowager's
fancy fur;
Let me be the sore,
on the calloused derriere of
Mr. Bore.
Let me be the itch,
itching Miss Filthy Rich Bitch;
And let me be the pest,
in Old Mr. Buzzard's foul
feathered nest!

NO POET NEED APPLY

No poet need apply
to the Redwhiteandblue employ-
ment agency.
No boat rockers; no trouble-
making whistle blowers will do.
Wanted: only tried and proven
true-blue: flag waving, horn
tooting; high falutin', bull
shooting; banner flying, button
wearing, slogan slinging yahoo,
from old Yazoo!
No poet need ever apply
to the pieintheskybyandbye
company.
No poet's finger in the pot,
that would spoil the whole lot.
Needed: only Bible thumping,
soapbox stumping, joy juice
pumping to fit the moral immoral
majority. Mom's prize winning
apple pie,
is just not the apple of the
poets' hungry eye.
And this sweet joy juice,
peachy creamy, well
that is just not the poets'
cup of tea.
No poet ever ever need apply
to the VIP university.
He has not yet earned his
blue blooded pedigree in bull-
shitski.
No domesticated pet of the
sophisticated set,

no tail wagging puppy dog of
the literati.
To the quid pro quo of the
status quo, the poet's one dirty
so-and-so, a real no-no.
From the business-as-usual
One of Us Club, the poet always
gets the cold shoulder snub.
The poet is certainly no VIP
to the powers who be.
Their fondest wish that he
R.I.P.

WRITING POETRY

I heard a poet say; in his own poetical way:
"Writing poetry is just as simple as A, B, C!
Always Be Creative, see?
Use a good measure of metaphor and simile.
Mix in a good part of word play.
And now you have poetry!
According to the poet;
poetry is just as easy as A,B,C.
To the mathematician; it's like 1,2,3!
Always Be Creative; but, always be critical
of what is; and of what may be.
This is the heart and soul of poetry!
Never! No never ever; accept the status quo!
Oh no! NO! NO! NO!
It is the very lifeblood of poetry;
to challenge inevitability!
This gives the poet; and his poetry
legitimate credibility!
Poetry is just as simple; and as easy;
as A,B,C; it's like 1,2,3!
That's the poet's way!
There is little more to say!
Always Be Creative; Always Be Critical;
Always Be Colorful! In what you have to say.
Write colorful phrases using interesting
words that just love to play!
You will write; you will create;
a very poetic; a very lyrical poetic lay!

THE POET IN US

Each one of us has a space in time;
each one of us has a place in time;
it is the purpose of the poet
in each one of us;
to write some reason;
into our season of rhyme!
To try and make sense out of all this nonsense!
To add just a little meaning;
just a little bit of purpose;
with our very own memorable line!

ONLY FEEL*

You can be taught to believe.
You can be taught what to believe.
You can be taught how to believe.
You can be taught to know.
You can be taught what to know.
You can be taught how to know.
You can be taught to speak.
You can be taught when to speak.
You can be taught how to speak.
You can be taught what to say.
You can be taught to think.
You can be taught what to think.
You can be taught how to think.
You cannot be taught to feel.
You cannot be taught what to feel.
You cannot be taught how to feel.
What you believe. What you know.
What you say. What you think.
these are all borrowed from what
someone else has believed; has known;
has said; and has thought.
This is not your own.
You cannot claim it for your own.
You cannot in any way, call it your own.
It is not yours. For you, it is not real.
To you, it is unreal.
What you feel belongs to you.
It belongs to no one else but you.
What you feel is true. To you and only to you.
what you feel is very real.
It is real to you. It is real only for you.
What you feel makes you true.
It makes you true; especially to you.
It makes you seem real.

Makes you feel real, and true to others too.
Only when you feel, can you be truly true;
and really real, to yourself;
and true and real, to others too!
This is really true. So be true, and
only always true. Be real, and always
real; to be you and only always you!
To be true and real; only always true and
real; you must only and always feel!
* Suggested by a speech of e.e. cummings:
"Advice To A Poet…"

A POET LIFTS HIS PEN

A bird lifts it's wing,
preparing to fly;
then launches it's fragile
feathered craft,
upon an ocean of sky.
A poet lifts his pen,
preparing to write;
then sets sail upon
uncharted seas...
that invite! Excite! Incite!

POETRY RECIPE

Put pen to paper.
Then thought to pen.
This is the way a poet will begin.
Blend in meaty metaphor;
stir in some savory simile.
You have a simple recipe,
for cooking up poetry!
Then, add a little fantasy,
just for flavor.
Next a little alliteration,
for the ear to favor.
How about a fun pun,
with a bit of playful word play?
Now an original idea;
a creative thought.
Oh look what a poetic gift,
the poet has wrought!

THE POET'S WORLD

The poet live sin his dream world,
a world of fantasy.
Here what is not, can become is;
and what will not, will come to be.
In the poet's world, reality
can be changed; there is no inevitability.
Dreams do take root and grow.
In the poet's world of poetry,
this is true; this is so.
The poet's world is one of
rainbows in the mist; of starburst
nights, filled with harvest moons.
A merry May, chasing in play,
a young spring bride, June.
The voices of day, join with
the chorus of night;
in nature's serenade of dark and light.
This is Mother Nature's own sweet
symphony; her lovesong to the masses
of humanity.
This the poet's poetic paeon to poetry.

THE SURGEON

His pen in hand, the poet is a surgeon;
armed with his scalpel and sharp knife.
With his poet's pen, the poet dissects
the raw live flesh and blood body of life.
With a steady hand, he cuts out
a small part of his brain;
handing it to the reader, as a gourmet
chef would serve it up on a dish.
Do you want to know what I know?
Dear reader, is this your wish?
So, you want to know what I think?
Here, read my thoughts printed on
this paper, with pen and ink.
The poet then cuts out a chunk of his heart.
You want to know me heart and soul?
Well, here's a big part of my heart.
My soul and my mind,
are on this very page, you will find.
My dear reader, you will find me,
in these lines of poetry.

*e.e. he...

e.e., he
walked out into the fields of night sky
gathering poetry
plucking for his poetic bouquet
blossoms of starsilver
picking flowers of moongold a story that e. e. he
told and then retold
he sailed his frail craft the S.S. Poetry
through fogs of almostness
into the mists of poetry's restless sea
into morning's undiscovered new springland
where meadows of silver beauty lay silent
in twilights golden moments
past the witchcraft of experience
he sailed his fragile ship
through mysterious worlds of magic musery
where yes, the only lovely answer
ruled a kingdom of touchings
springing up from the earth's spontaneous
gladness joy never felt before
across so many many lands of unknowness he
journeyed to magical places
where cool faces of the wind kiss
soft hands of silent rain
in the early petals of sometime
he scented love's soft sweetness
there love beckoned him and wooed him
with her sensuous seductive melody
a pauper at beauty's door
he was welcomed to paint the
honeyed sweetness of her voice
to sculpt the poetic symmetry of her

perfectly formed body
here in love's own universe he
discovered her secrets and was made
witness to the masquerade that was
the charlatan's charade of so many
many empty dead souls
and too many comfortable minds
this much e. e. he did see
as he walked out and about the
starry fields of night
gathering his bright bouquets of poetry.
*In memory of e.e. cummings…

THE POET'S PURPOSE

To give voice to the voiceless.
Joy to the joyless.
Hope to the hopeless.
Love to the loveless!
To give the wingless wings.
To teach the songless to sing.
To help bear the heavy yoke
worn by humankind.
To plant the seed of a dream, in
some fertile mind.
To help the deaf hear.
To give sight to the blind.
To free the shackled souls;
those imprisoned and bound!
To give to man a keener eye;
a sharper ear; a longer reach.
To excite; incite; inspire each!
To give a helping hand; a welcome smile.
To reach down and lift up the down-trodden.
For at the very least; a short while.
To give an openness:
an open eye; an open ear; an open mind;
an open heart; an open door; an open life!
An open eye to see father and inwardly.
An open ear to hear clearly; distinctly.
An open mind to think wisely.
To dream often; to dream big.
An open heart to love fully; and freely!
An open door to greet and welcome all.
An open hand; open arms; an open life!
All of this to give the whole world!
To tell it just the way it was.

And to tell it just the way it is,
To tell it like it could be.
To tell it like it should be;
and just maybe like it ought to be!
This is the goal; and the role of the poet!
This is the purpose of poetry!

MR. POET

He called me, Mr. Poet;
and the sound of it, had a very nice ring.
Although I knew if there were a Mr. Poet,
then more than likely, I was not such a thing.
Still, I do like that name, Mr. Poet.
And I do want you to know it.
If it may not be my entitle, to claim it
as my title or name;
I do like it all the same.
And right now I don't know anyone,
who would have the nerve to dispute my claim.
So friend, if you wish, you may address
me as Mr. Poet; that is, if you want to.
And if you don't want to, I reckon that's
alright too.
Fr my friend, you see, it is quite an
honor for me;
to wear the name of Mr. Poet,
is to represent all poetry.
To me this is a far greater honor, than to be
given a doctoral degree;
from some high faluting university.

DON OF POETRY

The Man from La Mancha, Don Quixote;
you could say that Quixote was
THE "Don of Poetry!"
With his faithful steed; his trusty sword;
and Sancho Panza at his side;
each day the Don rode out;
to put the enemy to rout;
to battle injustice and stem
tyranny's tyrannical tide!
To confront the Goliath of hatred;
that awesome monster of Biblical lore;
armed only with his sharp pen;
he rides out to fight for his fellow men;
a modern day David; from those
ancient days of yore!
He goes forth to fight those ancient
monsters of ignorance and fear;
he rides forth into the fray;
to rid mankind of this cancer, and to
try to save the day.
And before it is too late;
to spare mankind from a more
tragic fate!

STAIRS

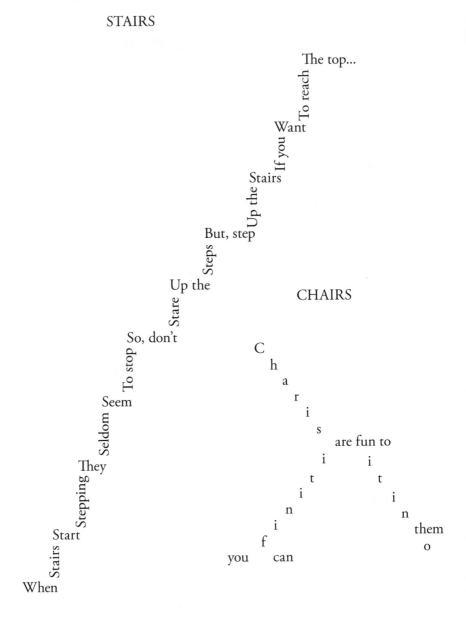

The top...
To reach
Want
If you
Stairs
Up the
But, step
Steps
Up the
Stare
So, don't
To stop
Seem
Seldom
They
Stepping
Start
Stairs
When

CHAIRS

C
h
a
r
i
s
are fun to
i   i
t   t
i   i
n   n   them
i   o
you   can
f

THE AUTHOR Tom

A Poem Is A Moving Thing..

Tom Hipps was born March 15, 1935, in Deering, Missouri. Son of a sharecrop cotton farmer, he grew up in Greenhill, Ala., graduating from Rogers High School in 1954. Graduating from David Lipscomb College in Nashville, Tenn., he earned his B.A. Degree in the spring of 1958.

Following graduation, he went to New Jersey to teach and has also taught in Tennessee and Pennsylvania. During the 1971-72 school year, Hipps served as "Poet In Residence", in Weakley County, Tennessee. This was under the "Poet In The Schools Program", sponsored by the Tennessee Arts Commission and the National Endowment for the Arts and Humanities.

Bill Martin, nationally known author and lecturer with Holt Rhinehart and Winston, describes Hipps' love poetry as "delicate and beautiful. "Chuck Stone, formerly with the Philadelphia Daily News, says of Hipps' poetry: "It is witty and though provoking... absolutely marvelous!"

Other collections by the author are: Moon Wine; Openings; A Gift of Wings; Cold Moons; The Shadow People; Main Street Muse; Poetically Yours; Jes Plain Folks; Nash Hash; Into The Winds; Children Of The Sun; The Book Of Thomas; Faces Of A Poet; A Lover's Quarrel; Touchings; When Worlds Were Young; You Me Poetry; A Poem Is A Moving Thing; The Poem And I; A Bone To Pick; The Child Within; Strife Street; Love Is; Cowpen Days; Philamusings; Philadaze; and Mumbo Jumbo Gumbo.

"Love's function is to fabricate unknownness."
e.e. cummings
Tom

"MY HEART HAS A THOUSAND SONGS TO SING..."